Advance Praise for

HOW TO SURVIVE DATING

"I'm not a fan of the "so-called" experts. What do they know? This is the first book (and series) that gives it to you straight from "real people" who have been there in the trenches. Unlike so many other self-help books, I actually read this one."

> —STEVE LINOWES
> WASHINGTON, D.C.

"A great handbook to one of life's best adventures. HUNDREDS OF HEADS sharing their wisdom. Practical, readable and fun."

> —J.R. WILLIAMSON
> ATLANTA, GEORGIA

"I couldn't put it down. The stories and advice are hilarious and wise. I can't wait to try some of this in the real world."

> —LESLIE KIMERLING
> NEW YORK, NEW YORK

"Everyone is trying to uncover the mystery of dating (and have some fun along the way). If your Eight Ball isn't working, this book is a great place to begin."

> —KEN HABER
> LOS ANGELES, CALIFORNIA

"The journey of dating can be a 5-star adventure or a slow windy hot bus ride. *How to Survive Dating* gives practical and authentic advice for finding love, or at least how to have fun while trying."

> —DEBRA AND KEN CHIZINSKY
> SANTA CRUZ, CALIFORNIA

WARNING:

This Guide contains differing
opinions. Hundreds of Heads
will not always agree.
Advice taken in combination may
cause unwanted side effects. Use
your Head when selecting advice.

How to Survive Dating

How to • Survive
Dating

by
Hundreds
of Happy
Singles
Who Did *

*and some things to avoid, from a few broken hearts who didn't

edited by
MARK W. BERNSTEIN AND YADIN KAUFMANN

Hundreds of Heads Books, Inc.

ATLANTA

Copyright © 2004 by Hundreds of Heads Books, Inc., Atlanta, GA

All rights reserved. No portion of this book may be reproduced—mechanically, electronically, or by any other means, including photocopying—without written permission of the publisher.

Trademarks: Hundreds of Heads, Because Hundreds of Heads are Better than One!, and related trade dress are trademarks or registered trademarks of Hundreds of Heads Books, Inc., and may not be used without written permission. All other trademarks are the property of their respective owners. Hundreds of Heads Books, Inc. is not associated with any product or vendor mentioned in this book.

Illustrations © 2004 by Image Club

Library of Congress Cataloging in Publication information on file.
See page 207 for credits and permissions.

Limit of Liability/Disclaimer of Warranty: Every effort has been made to accurately present the views expressed by the interviewees quoted herein. The publisher and editors regret any unintentional inaccuracies or omissions, and do not assume responsibility for the opinions of the respondents. The advice contained herein may not be suitable for your situation (in fact, some of it may be dangerous to your health!). Neither the publisher nor the authors of any of the stories herein shall be liable for any loss of profit or any other commercial damages, including but not limited to special, incidental, consequential, or other damages.

Cover and book design by Elizabeth Johnsboen

Cover photograph by Image Source
Interior illustrations by Image Club

HUNDREDS OF HEADS™ books are available at special discounts when purchased in bulk for premiums or institutional or educational use. Excerpts and custom editions can be created for specific uses. For more information, please email sales@hundredsofheads.com or write to:

HUNDREDS OF HEADS BOOKS, INC.
#230
2221 Peachtree Road, Suite D
Atlanta, GA 30309

ISBN 0-9746292-1-9

Printed in U.S.A.
10 9 8 7 6 5 4 3 2 1

CONTENTS

Introduction

Who among us has not spent countless hours analyzing—and overanalyzing—our dating situations? Should I ask her out? Should I call him back? Did I say the right thing? Should I call again? Should I let him pay? Will he really look like his Internet picture? When do I ask her to live with me? How do I get out of this one . . .

This book the second in the HUNDREDS OF HEADS™ Survival Guide series, grew out of the simple idea that when you're facing any of life's major challenges—such as navigating the treacherous currents of dating—it's good to get advice from people who have "been there, done that." Why make all the mistakes for yourself?

Other advice books, no matter how smart or expert their authors, are generally limited to the knowledge of only one person. This book takes a different approach: It assembles the experiences of hundreds of people, stalwart daters who play the dating game and——win or lose——emerge with some wisdom to share. If two heads are better than one, as the saying goes, then hundreds of them should be even better.

To create this book, we interviewed men and women from all over the country (and even a few from around the world). What they told us about their dating experiences—whether satisfied, relieved, or regretful—was remarkably universal. It confirmed that all of us encounter similar obstacles and oddities, pain and pleasure, fun and funniness, whatever our dating goals.

As you might expect, we heard many different views—and you'll often find opposite views on the same aspects of dating life: where to meet your next date, whether Internet dating works, who should pay, should we have sex, should we live together? You may not agree with a particular respondent's point of view, but in this book you can choose from hundreds of others. So read on. Armed with the wisdom of all these people, you may make fewer mistakes yourself and have more fun along the way.

MARK W. BERNSTEIN
YADIN KAUFMANN

SPECIAL THANKS

Thanks to our intrepid "headhunters" for going out to find so many daters from around the country with interesting advice to share:

Jamie Allen, Chief Headhunter

Lindsay Brillson	Natasha Lambropoulos	William Ramsey
Jennifer Blaise Kramer	Nicole Lessin	Kazz Regelman
Scott Deckman	Robin Lofton	Jennifer Bright Reich
Sara Faiwell	Lindsey R. Miller	Graciela Sholander
Marlene Goldman	Jennifer Nittoso	Laura Roe Stevens
Teena Hammond Gomez	Christina Orlovsky	Helen Trickey
Elizabeth Hockstad	Adam Pollock	Beth Turney
Lisa Jaffe Hubbell	Lisa Powell	Matt Twetten
Shannon Hurd	Pedro Ramirez III	Jade Walker
		Sara Walker

Thanks, too, to our editorial advisor Anne Kostick. And thanks to our assistant, Miri Greidi, for yeoman's work keeping us all organized.

The real credit for this book, of course, goes to all the people whose experiences and collective wisdom make up this guide. There are too many of you to thank individually, of course, but you know who you are. Thanks for sharing.

American Idol: What We're Looking For

I t seems most people in the dating world are searching for some-one—but whom? The answer differs with every dater. Whether you're in it for momentary fun or looking for a lifelong mate, it helps to be honest with yourself about your goals—and honest with others, too. Read on to discover what people want, what they don't want, and what they really, really don't want.

DATING IS LIKE SEARCHING FOR THE PERFECT WINE. One date is too fruity, another too dry, and still another too much bouquet (cologne overdose). But once you find the perfect variety that suits your taste, get drunk.

—KATIE KOSKO
PITTSBURGH, PENNSYLVANIA

THE CONCEPT OF DATING IS MUCH BETTER THAN THE PRACTICE.

—J.S.
NEW YORK,
NEW YORK

THERE ARE TWO KINDS OF DATING: The fun kind, purely for entertainment, and then the kind that's more serious. Be open about your intentions so no one gets hurt.

—*K.B.*
DANVILLE, CALIFORNIA

. . . .

"I only date men who don't speak English. That way, everything they say is funny, and very, very sexy."

—*ISABELLA*
CHAMPAIGN, ILLINOIS

. . . .

I like all flavors.

—*SARAH*
SEATTLE,
WASHINGTON

DON'T COMPROMISE IN YOUR SEARCH. I'm looking for the person who's going to make me want to be with her for the rest of my life. Compromise on the color of your car or the size of your house, but not on the girl you're going to be with the rest of your life.

—*RICHARD*
ATLANTA, GEORGIA

. . . .

I LIKE A WOMAN WHO IS SASSY AND SMART, does not wear a bathrobe, and can hold her own with a menu. A friend of mine shaved her boyfriend's head while he was passed out drunk. That's the kind of girl for me.

—*JONATHAN ADAMS*
SAN FRANCISCO, CALIFORNIA

IF A DATE CANNOT TAP INTO YOUR SENSE of humor—at least on the first date, when you are presumably on your best behavior—run away!

> —*A.R.T.*
> *SAN FRANCISCO, CALIFORNIA*

· · · · · · · ·

FIND SOMEBODY WHO'S HONEST, makes you laugh, and whom you have a good time with. Find someone you can fight with, act like you're five years old with, and also have an intelligent conversation with.

> —*KIM*
> *JACKSONVILLE, FLORIDA*

· · · · · · · ·

I'LL GLADLY TAKE BLUNT OR CRASS OVER DISCREET and well mannered if it means we're able to communicate well. I don't believe in an afterlife, and I've got lots of things I'd like to do in my one lifetime. I can't afford to waste any time playing games.

> —*CHAD MAKAIO ZICHTERMAN*
> *SAN FRANCISCO, CALIFORNIA*

· · · · · · · ·

MANY WOMEN ARE LOOKING FOR A HUSBAND, and if you don't want to be one you should let them know that as early as you can. Don't let her think you are going to be her Prince Charming if all you want to be is her Night Jester.

> —*KEITH MCCARTHY*
> *PITTSBURGH, PENNSYLVANIA*

· · · · · · · ·

I DON'T REALLY DATE GIRLS TO BE SERIOUS. We just hang out and have fun, and when we stop having fun then we part ways. Try to keep things simple.

> —*AARON*
> *DULUTH, GEORGIA*

Dating is so much fun; don't rush to get married.

> —*BEATRICE*
> *MIAMI, FLORIDA*

If he says "Nuke-yoo-ler," I'm not interested.

> —*N.*
> *BROOKLYN, NEW YORK*

QUALIFIED APPLICANTS ONLY

I made a list of qualities I'm attracted to in others. Must-haves are: A sense of humor; has made peace with his past; and good dental hygiene. There are also desirables that I don't expect anyone to ever have all of, but man, if he did, I'd be flabbergasted, and hooked for sure:

1) does not tell jokes that start out, "A man, a donkey, and the Pope walk into a bar..."
2) is a great leader
3) keeps a clean house
4) is strong but gentle with strength
5) is interested in music and the arts
6) is courteous, fearless, kind, and dignified
7) knows when to be silent and listen
8) is filled with a religion that has no origins in books, creeds, or observations
9) has a desire to help those that have the need or desire for help
10) is spontaneous, athletic, wise, and humble
11) is respectful of nature
12) enjoys when other people succeed
13) is both masculine and feminine
14) is politically inclined
15) is open-minded to new experiences and likes adventure
16) is romantic, imaginative, and gives love freely
17) is ever-evolving
18) contributes to a better world every day in some way
19) lives in the present
20) challenges my thinking
21) liked Van Halen better when Dave was in the band
22) is dependable.

—ZOE
PHOENIX, ARIZONA

I'M LOOKING FOR A READER. I don't have to have everything in common with the man I meet, but I love reading. Someone who prioritizes reading; I like that.

— *N.B.*
  OAKLAND, CALIFORNIA

• • • • • • • •

I'D LIKE TO MEET A GIRL who has nice, clean, long fingernails, so she can scratch my scalp and back.

— *MIKE*
  CHICO, CALIFORNIA

• • • • • • • •

 DRUG AND/OR ALCOHOL ABUSE, FELONIES, lies, violence, passive aggression, laziness, intellectual flaccidity, and an absence of sexual chemistry are deal-breakers for me. Shouldn't they be deal-breakers for everyone? Why would you date a guy who's high or cheating or chronically unemployed or bad in bed? How is this preferable to being single?

— *LITSA DREMOUSIS*
  SEATTLE, WASHINGTON

• • • • • • • •

DON'T BE AFRAID TO JUMP IN THE DATING POOL and find out about people and yourself. Sort it out, and you'll know what you need to know when the right person comes along.

— *LINDA*
  LOS ANGELES, CALIFORNIA

• • • • • • • •

YOU SHOULD DATE SOMEONE you are physically attracted to. This may sound shallow, but it is much easier to put up with minor irritations when you feel that attraction.

— *KIRAN*
  ATLANTA, GEORGIA

I'm very tall. It really doesn't work for me to date someone shorter than five-ten.

— *G.R.*
  SACRAMENTO, CALIFORNIA

If he asks to borrow money, forget it.

— *KAREN*
  NEW YORK, NEW YORK

Humor me.
That's my
slogan.

—*Shirley*
Suisun City,
California

Look for friendship first, because we all have different criteria when we date. We look for what the media tells us is "right": Tall, dark, handsome, and rich in a man; slender, blonde, and beautiful in a woman. But when we think in terms of friendship, we center on similar values such as trust, sense of humor, honesty, and communication skills. We are more forgiving of our friends, and these friendships often develop into a more serious relationship.

—*Elaine Fantle Shimberg* *
Tampa, Florida

*(see credits page 207)

WOW!

I like unexpected kisses, like when a guy can't contain himself and just leans over and kisses me while I'm in mid-sentence, or when we're in a public place. I place a lot of value on kissing. Basically there are three kinds of kisses: One, the wrong kind, where you're not attracted to the other person and they kiss you and you realize how truly gross kissing is. Two, someone kisses you that you think is great but you realize you have no chemistry. It's nice but it doesn't knock your socks off. Then there's the "wow" kiss. That's when someone kisses you and you feel that electric charge shoot through your body. I live for "wow" kissing. It's my favorite drug.

—*Haley*
Atlanta, Georgia

THERE ARE MANY STAGES OF DATING: dating seriously but not exclusively; dating exclusively but not seriously; dating seriously and exclusively; not dating seriously or exclusively.

—*ALLIE R.*
WASHINGTON, D.C.

- - - - - - - -

KEEP YOUR STANDARDS HIGH and never waiver. Why waste your time on someone you have no interest in?

—*JANIS BLAISE*
DIABLO, CALIFORNIA

- - - - - - - -

IF YOU GO ACTIVELY LOOKING for the love of your life you will never find him or her. Most of the time it just happens by accident.

—*JOHN BARANYAI*
MELBOURNE, AUSTRALIA

- - - - - - - -

LONELINESS IS NO EXCUSE FOR COMPROMISE. Be comfortable with yourself before you choose to be with someone else just to avoid being alone.

—*CRISTOFFER L.*
SAN DIEGO, CALIFORNIA

- - - - - - - -

ALMOST ALL OF MY BOYFRIENDS HAVE STARTED as close friends, and it's been a mutually slow, involved process. I always want to be inspired to make the first move, but I don't have the guts. So I just put energy out there that shows I'm receptive to a move.

—*MARIA*
ASHEVILLE, NORTH CAROLINA

I'm dating a karate teacher. But he can't be my karate teacher because I don't respect him enough.

—*J.*
SAN JUAN,
PUERTO RICO

I like poets, especially poetesses.

—*MARK*
SAN FRANCISCO,
CALIFORNIA

FRIENDLY FACES

DON'T BE AFRAID TO DATE YOUR BEST FRIEND, because that's whom you should marry.

> —*FRAN WILLS*
> *LITTLETON, COLORADO*

• • • • • • • •

I DON'T KNOW IF IT'S POSSIBLE TO DATE A FRIEND. Guys never look at women as friends. If she's good-looking and he's single, there's always a scoopaloopa in mind.

> —*PANOS KOUTSOYANNIS*
> *SAN FRANCISCO, CALIFORNIA*

• • • • • • • • •

I LIKE MEETING POTENTIAL BOYFRIENDS THROUGH FRIENDS—it's like having a built-in reference.

> —*L.B.B.*
> *MONTREAL, QUEBEC, CANADA*

• • • • • • • • •

I THINK IT'S BETTER TO DATE SOMEONE YOU ALREADY KNOW as a friend because you are already familiar with them and it makes it easier to maintain a relationship with them. If you are going to be involved with dating someone, I believe you should count them as a friend before you count them as a lover.

> —*BEV WALTON-PORTER*
> *COLORADO SPRINGS, COLORADO*

• • • • • • • • •

I OFTEN DATE SOMEONE WHO WAS A FRIEND FIRST. I do this because I'm cautious about opening up nowadays, and by knowing him for a while as a friend, I get a wider range of knowledge about him than I would if I just started dating him.

> —*CHRISTINA*
> *BELMONT, MASSACHUSETTS*

A Really Big Haystack: Where to Find Someone Special

W*e know you're not desperate. But still, it wouldn't hurt to go somewhere and meet someone nice, would it? Is that too much to ask? We think not. After all, there's no shortage of people looking for that special connection. But where should you go to improve your odds? Read on to see what worked for others.*

I FOUND MOST OF MY DATES AT 7-ELEVEN. I dated a policeman, a doctor, a lawyer, and I met my husband there. Talk about your convenience. My husband was a soldier and a truck driver; I swore I'd never marry either: I married both.

—*TERRY PEZZELLA*
BEL AIR, MARYLAND

THERE ARE POTENTIAL DATES EVERYWHERE.

—*ZOE*
PHOENIX, ARIZONA

WHERE'S THE BEST PLACE TO FIND A HUSBAND?

College. Why? Well, you are on a similar path of pursuing a degree. And you can meet the other person's friends, which helps to place them in some context so you can learn more about them. If you dislike your boyfriend's friends, it is a good sign that you don't have much in common with your boyfriend. I met my husband in college. We were both pursuing our professional goals: He wanted to be a dentist, and I wanted to be a psychologist. Also, we had many of the same friends.

—*M.S.L.*
WAIKOLOA, HAWAII

• • • • • • • •

YOU HAVE TO BE YOURSELF

and be completely content with what you are doing. And you'll find that when you're not looking for someone, and when you're happier alone, that's when they come to you.

—*LILY*
SEATTLE, WASHINGTON

• • • • • • • •

BE NICE TO EVERYONE YOU DATE

because you never know whom they might know. Many times I will go out with a woman and things will not work out. But then, the girl will introduce me to all her friends and I hit the jackpot.

—*MOSHEI KATZ*
MONSEY, NEW YORK

• • • • • • • •

PARTIES ARE NOT THAT DIFFERENT FROM BARS,

but bars are full of people who are trying to get back at their exes. At parties, there's the assumption that you have mutual friends and it's the reason you're both there. It opens the door for conversation.

—*DIRK*
ATLANTA, GEORGIA

If you're not good at meeting people, go places with a friend who is good at starting conversations with the opposite sex.

—*S.A.F.*
TAMPA, FLORIDA

BEFORE I WENT AWAY TO SCHOOL, my mother told me that college was a smorgasbord of good-looking guys; that once I went to college, there would be this line of attractive, available men for me to choose from. So I came to school, and I met lots of good-looking guys, lots of available guys—and not a single one I'd consider dating. College boys are one or the other—hot or available. If you find one who happens to be a combination of the two, hold on to him like it's your job. I've almost graduated, and I'm still looking for that smorgasbord.

> —*ERIN P.*
> *COLUMBIA, MISSOURI*

. . . .

IF YOU FEEL LIKE YOU'RE NOT MEETING any new people, go to new places and try new things. There are always more people out there to date. You have to find them or help them find you. Keep an open mind. When you meet someone new, don't be in a hurry to decide if he is right for you, give yourself a chance to get to know him.

> —*ELOISE MILLIKEN*
> *CALIFON, NEW JERSEY*

. . . .

I ALWAYS TOOK THE PHILOSOPHY that the more people you meet, the percentage increases that you'll meet someone who you'll really connect with and perhaps have a long-term relationship with.

> —*MICHELE*
> *WALNUT CREEK, CALIFORNIA*

Don't knock a free ride from a stranger; that's how I found my man. That stranger might be the man or woman of your dreams.

> —*BRIDGETT BARLOW*
> *STREET, MARYLAND*

THREE RULES TO FINDING SOMEONE TO DATE: Don't be afraid to date your friends; don't date who your parents tell you to; and don't date someone at the office unless you think you may marry them, in which case it's fine. I met my husband at the office.

—*ANGI RASSI*
MINNEAPOLIS, MINNESOTA

• • • • • • • •

CHURCH IS THE BEST PLACE TO MEET a potential husband. I met my husband in church, though I wasn't looking for a husband at the time. But what better way to know if you share the same values and beliefs than to meet at a place of worship?

—*JAYNE J.*
TULSA, OKLAHOMA

• • • • • • • •

We met at the dog run. He had a golden retriever, I had a shepherd mix. All four of us clicked immediately.

—*J.*
SAN JUAN,
PUERTO RICO

GO TO REUNIONS—HIGH SCHOOL, COLLEGE, whatever. I know so many people that have ended up marrying or at least seriously dating somebody they re-met at a reunion. And let me tell you, it's never the person they dated in high school or even liked in high school. It's always somebody they would never have thought twice about.

—*SUSAN*
CHICAGO, ILLINOIS

• • • • • • • •

KEEP YOUR EYES, AND MIND, OPEN. You may find a great boyfriend in the most unlikely place. I had to drive a co-worker to work for a while after he broke his leg. We got to talk a lot and to know each other pretty well, and we ended up dating. He's now my husband.

—*M.B.*
SAN FRANCISCO, CALIFORNIA

I ONCE SAW SOME CUTE GUYS coming out of a building after work and walking down the street. I literally ran around the block so that I could "accidentally" bump into them head-on. Sure enough, they invited me to get some drinks with them, and I ended up going on a couple dates with one of them. The "accidental" bump is a good one, if you can pull it off naturally.

> —ANNE B.
> SAN FRANCISCO, CALIFORNIA

" The best place to meet someone is Italy. That country is the perfect place to fall in love. "

> —J.A.B.
> SAN FRANCISCO, CALIFORNIA

THE BEST WAY TO MEET PEOPLE IS not to go to bars or clubs: volunteer at a shelter or a park cleanup instead. There you get to see people in a different light (and also in daylight!). Under these circumstances, you can see if a person is a hard worker or lazy, and also how he works and plays with others.

> —JENNY
> DENTON, TEXAS

WHEN I GO OUT WITH MY GIRLFRIENDS, they can always tell if I got my paycheck or not by how low-cut my shirt is. My shirt gets lower as my need for free drinks increases.

> —V.B.
> NEW YORK, NEW YORK

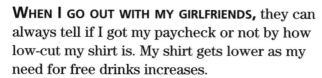

If I'm feeling flirty, I don't care where I am: I flirt. A smile and a wink work magic.

—ZOE
PHOENIX, ARIZONA

I MET MY WIFE SHOEING HORSES on the Bicentennial wagon train when it came through my town in the Shenandoah Valley.

—PAUL LONG
NEW HOPE, VIRGINIA

• • • • • • • •

IF YOU FOLLOW YOUR INTERESTS, you will be surrounded by people who share them. My parents' advice on dating was always to get involved with something you are really interested in. They met in their 30s, singing in the same Bach B-minor Mass.

—DAN
HELOTES, TEXAS

• • • • • • • •

BEST PLACE TO MEET WOMEN? It's coincidentally also the best place to meet men—conventions! These are great places to meet people with similar interests and to spend time mingling. And there won't be any loud music, so you can talk.

—DOUG LOFTON
WAIKOLOA, HAWAII

• • • • • • • •

THE BEST PLACE TO FIND SOMEONE is through "mitzvah therapy," which means doing good works. When you're working side-by-side on a Habitat for Humanity home, at a humane society, or volunteering in a hospital or at a performing arts center, you don't worry about your appearance or being clever. There's no pressure. You're having fun and know you're helping someone else.

—ELAINE FANTLE SHIMBERG*
TAMPA, FLORIDA

*(see credits page 207)

TRY TAKING A CLASS. My cousin swore by things like taking ballet as a college phys ed course because guys were few and far between, but lots of women signed up. I don't think you have to go that far, in part because if you take something you don't really like, you're more likely to end up looking desperate.

> —SCOTT TOBIN
> LOS ANGELES, CALIFORNIA

· · · · · · · ·

✓ **MEET PEOPLE THROUGH VOLUNTEERING.**
First of all, helping others makes you feel good, and of course, you're so busy being absorbed in an activity (hopefully with like-minded others) that you are much more likely to relax, be yourself, and you won't have time to experience dating jitters. I also suggest that people do activities that they really like (walking tours, weekend trips, tennis, golf), because if you're happy and interested in what you're doing, you're much more likely to relax and be yourself.

> —ALISON BLACKMAN DUNHAM
> BROOKLYN, NEW YORK

· · · · · · · ·

I MET THIS BEAUTIFUL BLONDE on top of a dam in Marin County, California, while changing a flat tire during a long road-biking session. She stopped to ask if I had everything I needed, which turned out to be a symbolic question.

> —A.R.T.
> SAN FRANCISCO, CALIFORNIA

· · · · · · · ·

DO NOT EVER DATE PEOPLE YOUR FRIENDS TRY to hook you up with, because it is always awkward and can get really uncomfortable later on.

> —JAN S.
> NEW YORK, NEW YORK

If you want a way to meet warm, caring women, get a dog and walk him in the park.

> —MARK
> SAN FRANCISCO,
> CALIFORNIA

IT HELPS TO KNOW THE WORDS

Men, sacrifice yourself on the altar of dignity. I have found that a willingness to make a fool of yourself shows two things to women: you're fun and you're confident. Whether you're trying to meet a girl, or you're on a first date, or on your 25th date, a playful side will always come off well—as long as you embarrass yourself and not her.

Once, I was at a karaoke bar in San Francisco and I was talking to a girl to whom a friend had introduced me. We were having a good conversation and we were both talking about how our friends dragged us to the karaoke bar and how neither of us liked to get up onstage and sing. After a couple of drinks someone got up and did a stirring rendition of some Michael Jackson song that got the whole place cheering, including the girl I was talking with. I realized I liked this girl, so on my next trip to the bathroom I very nervously put my name on the list. I walked back to the bar, made sure to order a stiff drink, and when they called my name, I winked at the girl and walked up onstage, exploding into the worst rendition of a Marvin Gaye classic that has ever graced the ears of mankind. All my friends were laughing and so was the girl I was trying to impress.

Once the song was over, as everyone congratulated me, I saw her smiling at me while she was talking to her friend. I took her out later that week and we have been dating ever since (almost two years). To this day, every time we walk by a karaoke bar she starts singing my song and I glow with the knowledge that a little self-deprecation goes a long way.

—JEREMY
SAN FRANCISCO, CALIFORNIA

I HAVE A FRIEND WHO HAS GREAT ADVICE about finding girls: Live with girls. Get one as a roommate. They are always cleaner, and they bring other girls around. He's had a lot of dates—all her friends.

—*JEREMY FORCÉ*
BOSTON, MASSACHUSETTS

• • • • • • • •

I MET A CUTE GIRL ONCE IN THE DMV LINE. It was awesome. We had two hours to get to know each other before I asked her out on a date. I guess traffic school could potentially be a good place to meet someone, too—at least you know you have something in common.

—*BILL*
SACRAMENTO, CALIFORNIA

• • • • • • • •

IF YOU'RE IN A RUT, YOU'RE GUARANTEED to meet someone if you go out of town. It happens to me all the time. But beware: long-distance relationships may be the result.

—*K.D.K.*
CHICAGO, ILLINOIS

• • • • • • • •

✔ **IT'S A NUMBERS GAME, JUST LIKE ANYTHING** else—sales, direct mail, etc. The more people you meet, the greater your odds of matching.

—*ANONYMOUS*
NEW YORK, NEW YORK

• • • • • • • •

THE WEIRDEST PLACE I'VE EVER MET SOMEONE was at a mortuary. I was there for the funeral of a friend and this beautiful woman was working the front desk. I asked her out.

—*BAKER*
ATLANTA, GEORGIA

5 BEST CITIES FOR DATING

You may be one of the lucky residents of these cities. If not, consider relocating.

1. Austin, Texas
2. Colorado Springs, Colorado
3. San Diego, California
4. Raleigh/Durham, North Carolina
5. Seattle, Washington

GOING TO THE GYM SERVES A DUAL PURPOSE. It really is great way to meet people. Everyone is primed to meet: people are constantly checking other people out.

—*S.H.*
YUBA CITY, CALIFORNIA

• • • • • • • •

ONE OF THE BEST PLACES FOR MEETING WOMEN is the grocery store. At the one I go to, there is nothing but hot women. They're not on defense there, like they are at a bar. They're more like themselves, too. They're not dressed up and they look more like they do every day. I'll open the conversation with a woman by giving her cooking tips. If I'm standing at the fish counter, I say; "Have you ever tried to cook it this way?" They immediately think, "Hey, he can cook." And they also think you're really nice. It impresses them.

—*MIKE*
SARASOTA, FLORIDA

DATES: THEY'RE ALWAYS IN THE LAST PLACE YOU LOOK

The most unexpected place for a woman to meet a guy to date is at a gay bar. I usually like going to gay bars to dance because you don't get hit on and you can let your defenses down. One time I went with my friends and I met a guy who I assumed was gay because, well, he was there. I was really friendly and chatty with him, but as it turned out he was a straight guy who had been dragged there (no pun intended) by his friends. He was a sweet guy and we ended up dating for six months.

—*LISA*
MINNEAPOLIS, MINNESOTA

I LIKE TO MEET GIRLS IN THE PARK. You see people jogging, you see different kinds of people there. If I see a girl I like (hopefully with a dog) I compliment the dog and then start a conversation with her.

—BIG J.
TAIPEI, TAIWAN

. . . .

I MET A WOMAN WHEN I WAS IN COSTUME at Halloween. We had some rapport, but my entire head and face were painted blue so she couldn't really tell what I looked like. Then I met her another night at a bar. As soon as I walked in I could tell that when she looked at me, she said to herself, "He's balding." It was pretty much over at that point.

—E.R.
ATLANTA, GEORGIA

. . . .

❝It's never a good idea to kiss a guy whose name you don't know. That's not the best way to get a date.❞

—AMANDA ANDERSEN
SAN DIEGO, CALIFORNIA

I WENT OVER TO THIS GIRL'S HOUSE to buy a box spring from her that she'd advertised on the Internet. I thought there might be some kind of chemistry between us, so I e-mailed her that same week. Six months later she e-mailed me back, and we dated for a little while.

—PHIL S.
SAN FRANCISCO, CALIFORNIA

IN ALL THE WRONG PLACES

IT'S HARD TO MEET MISTER OR MISS RIGHT AT A BAR. Unfortunately, that's what a lot of people try to do. The place to meet Mister or Miss Right is in church.

—*S.S.*
VIRGINIA BEACH, VIRGINIA

. . . .

GOING TO A BAR IS A WASTE OF TIME. What are the odds you're going to meet The One at a bar? If you like scuba diving, meet people scuba diving. If you like hiking, meet someone there. You're more likely to meet someone who's compatible while doing something you like.

—*ANONYMOUS*
NEW YORK, NEW YORK

. . . .

BEST PLACES TO MEET MEN? Nightclubs! Men who go to nightclubs are often looking for a relationship. Men who go to bars are just looking for sex. But men who go to hear good jazz are often the kinds who are looking to settle down.

—*CARMEN*
OAKLAND, CALIFORNIA

. . . .

THE BEST PLACE TO MEET MEN IS AT BARS. Church is no good because most people are already married. But to meet a lot of single men, go to a bar. It's all a numbers game. Eventually, you'll meet a nice guy who is looking for someone just like you. I met my husband, Dan, in a bar. I went with a friend who is a transsexual. She/he was interested in Dan first. My friend really flirted with Dan, but he wasn't interested in her. He only wanted to meet me. We're all still good friends.

—*M.R.*
VALLEJO, CALIFORNIA

I DATE REALLY CRAPPY GUYS AND I MEET THEM ALL IN BARS. I'm attracted to them for some reason and they end up losing their jobs, and then they lose their house or apartment, and then they need a place to stay. And I end up taking care of them. It's a repeating cycle.

—*KEIRSTIN*
FINDLEY, OHIO

BARS ARE FILLED WITH DRUNKEN IDIOTS. If you meet someone at a bar, they're just going to sleep with you and you'll never see them again.

—*KAYZE*
BALTIMORE, MARYLAND

I'M KIND OF SHY, SO I LIKE TO MEET GIRLS IN BARS. You can get a drink and that helps. It's a fun place to meet girls. But if you're looking to seriously date, maybe not.

—*JON WILLIAMS*
CHICAGO, ILLINOIS

 I DON'T MEET GIRLS IN BARS. The girls who try to talk to you in bars are looking for something else besides a date.

—*JIMMY JAMES*
GARY, INDIANA

I MEET A LOT OF PEOPLE WHEN I'VE BEEN DRINKING: that's what drinking does to me. I'm very flirtatious. I lose my inhibitions. I just go up to guys and say hello. Or I comment on something about them; what they're wearing or who they look like.

—*S.A.F.*
TAMPA, FLORIDA

THE ULTIMATE PLACE TO FIND DATES

I HAVE MET MOST OF THE PEOPLE I'VE DATED through Ultimate Frisbee, or at a teaching conference.

> —*ALYSON*
> *ATLANTA, GEORGIA*

• • • • • • • • •

I MET MY WIFE ON TOP OF A SOCCER GOAL. It was an Ultimate Frisbee tournament near Seattle, where I was visiting for a week of vacation. Our team had been knocked out of the tournament and a friend and I watched the finals from atop a soccer goal. I looked to my left and there, standing dozens of yards away, was a pretty young waif, watching her neighbor play in the big game. After a little eye-tickling with each other, I invited her to join me on top of the goal. Surprisingly, she accepted. It took me a little while, but by the third date that week, I knew that I wanted her to be my wife. The moral: If you are feeling down, look up. Your mate might be there.

> —*ANONYMOUS*
> *SANTA ROSA, CALIFORNIA*

TAKE ADVANTAGE OF YOUR SURROUNDINGS. I live in Hawaii. People who book package tours to Hawaii will often include a flower-lei greeting in their package. My friend and I used to work for a company that provides these greetings. In order to greet the proper visitors, we would get a passenger-arrival list at the beginning of the day and peruse the list for the "Ms." passengers. Our line would be, "Let us know if you need someone to show you around the island." A number of women took us up on our offer.

—*EDWARD BARINQUE*
EWA BEACH, HAWAII

• • • • • • • •

I HAVE HAD SUCCESS WITH DATING PEOPLE I knew previously from high school or college. This is ideal because I have a history with these people as friends and acquaintances, and that makes things more comfortable from the beginning.

—*BEV WALTON-PORTER*
COLORADO SPRINGS, COLORADO

The best place to meet a man is at a place you enjoy. I met my future husband at a car race.

—*NICOLE LIVEZY*
PITMAN,
NEW JERSEY

• • • • • • • •

IF YOU PLAN AND WORK TOO HARD, you'll never find the right person. I live my life, do things I enjoy and eventually trip over someone interesting. I met my current partner at a music festival. It's ideal because you are relaxed and being yourself, not manufacturing some persona you think someone will find attractive. It's too much like a bad job interview otherwise.

—*J.A.*
DURHAM, NORTH CAROLINA

5 WORST CITIES FOR DATING

Give yourself extra credit if you're happily dating in one of these cities:

1. Kansas City, Missouri

2. Wichita, Kansas

3. Minneapolis-St. Paul, Minnesota

4. Detroit, Michigan

5. Louisville, Kentucky

LOOK FOR DATES AT WORK, BUT DON'T PLAN to work with them for long. When you work with people you get the opportunity to learn about them as human beings. You see them stressed, happy, and so forth. It lets you form a friendship before things get heavier. Just know that if things do get more intense, one of you has got to go.

—SARAH
SEATTLE, WASHINGTON

• • • • • • • •

SUPERMARKETS ARE ALWAYS A GOOD PLACE to talk to women. I was once flirting with this woman, then I passed her a few aisles later and we had a football toss with a loaf of bread. I handed her the bread, ran down the aisle, shouted, "I'm open!" She threw it to me, I did a victory lap around the next aisle, and ran back to her. It was a fun way to talk to someone I thought was attractive.

—DAVE
STOCKTON, CALIFORNIA

• • • • • • • •

I MET MY FORMER FIANCÉE AT A BUS STOP. That isn't so strange, but we met because we both loved Sesame Street and randomly started singing the words to "The People in Your Neighborhood" at the same time.

—CHAD MAKAIO ZICHTERMAN
SAN FRANCISCO, CALIFORNIA

• • • • • • • •

DON'T FOCUS ON DATING. Focus on doing things that make you happy. Find activities that you're passionate about and do those things and you have a better chance of meeting someone there, when you're not looking. Don't do activities to meet a guy. Focus on making yourself happy.

—PEGGY
ST. PETERSBURG, FLORIDA

IN ANY LANGUAGE, JUST AS BAD

Agreeing to go out with someone you meet after consuming a few drinks in a bar isn't always the best idea. If you think you like someone, try to have a little more contact with them before committing to the dinner date. I met this guy in a bar: he was from Bolivia. When he came over to talk to me it was very loud and his English wasn't that great, but hey, I'd had a few drinks, so I agreed to go out with him. When he came to pick me up, I realized he barely spoke English. It was much worse than it seemed at the bar. He took me to a nice restaurant. He asked me what I was going to have. I said, "Salmon." He gave me a strange look, then ordered swordfish for both of us. Did he not understand me? Is that a Bolivian custom, or did he just decide what I wanted wasn't good enough? Two days later, he sent me a big bouquet at work, with a card that read, "I feel like I've known you forever." I've been dodging him ever since.

—*Amber Sundsted*
Naples, Florida

ME: THE ABRIDGED VERSION

SPEED DATING IS BECOMING POPULAR WHERE I LIVE. You go to a place with other people your age. You spend eight minutes talking to one person, then you rotate and talk with someone else. This goes on until you've met everyone. At the end of the night, everyone lists the people they'd like to get to know, and the facilitators match you up.

—*CAROL*
EASTON, PENNSYLVANIA

SPEED DATING DOESN'T GIVE YOU ENOUGH TIME to get to know someone. Hanging out in coffee shops works much better for meeting people and starting conversations. In fact, a job interview is easier than speed dating! In a job interview, you have 30 minutes or more to explain who you are and show what you can do. In speed dating, you have just three minutes.

—*ROBERT*
CHICAGO, ILLINOIS

SPEED DATING IS MORE INTERESTING TO ME than online dating services because it's easier to learn more about someone. With the Internet, you never know if the other person is being honest about his looks, his career, or his age. With speed dating, you meet maybe 20 different men in a span of a few hours and know right away if you're compatible or not. At most of the speed dating events I've been to, the women sit at a table and the men rotate every five minutes, introducing themselves and making small talk. At the end, everyone writes down who they liked and if you select someone and they've selected you as well, then it's a match, and the coordinator of the event gives the woman the man's phone number. That way the woman can decide if she wants to call him or not. There is no pressure and everyone is always very nice.

—*J.*
CHICAGO, ILLINOIS

THE THING ABOUT DATING is that it's hardly ever called a date. It's "let's hang out," "let's get together," "let's get some food," or "let's go get some beers." Those are all ways of asking someone out for a date. If someone says, "let's hang out," it's a casual way to ask someone out. Be assertive. Ask people if they want to get together or hang out.

—*SYLVIA HOWELL*
BERKELEY, CALIFORNIA

● ● ● ● ● ● ● ● ●

"Don't think you can't live by yourself until you've tried it. Be independent and be picky about whom you date. Don't date the first person that comes along. Being single is OK."

—*MARI G.*
AZUSA, CALIFORNIA

● ● ● ● ● ● ● ● ●

THERE'S NO HARM IN ASKING SOMEONE for a date. There was a woman I was interested in at work, but I knew she had a boyfriend. I didn't know how serious they were, and I figured even a rejection couldn't hurt me. She said "No, I'm pretty serious with my boyfriend, but I'm flattered." I actually felt better that at least I had tried. And also, I figured if they did break up, she would know I was interested.

—*TONY T.*
SAN FRANCISCO, CALIFORNIA

THERE'S NO "BEST PLACE" TO MEET MISTER RIGHT.
There's only Mister Right! I met the man I married when I was on vacation in Israel. At the end of the vacation, he asked for my phone number, then introduced me to his friend as his future wife. Ten months later we moved in together.

—*BEATRICE*
MIAMI, FLORIDA

• • • • • • • •

I'VE TRIED ONLINE DATING, PERSONAL ADS, and blind chance, as well as blind dates, and I have had the best luck with meetings that grew out of common interests: writer's conferences, writer's groups, auditions for theater.

—*J. M. CORNWELL*
TABERNASH, COLORADO

MOVIES TO PUT YOU IN THE MOOD

Rent one of these top-rated movies by the American Film Institute for a home date. Add microwave popcorn and see what happens!

1. Casablanca (1942)
2. Gone with the Wind (1939)
3. West Side Story (1961)
4. Roman Holiday (1953)
5. An Affair to Remember (1957)
6. The Way We Were (1973)
7. Dr. Zhivago (1965)
8. It's a Wonderful Life (1946)
9. Love Story (1970)
10. City Lights (1931)

GROUP DYNAMICS

EVERY TIME I'M ON A TRIP WITH MY GIRLFRIENDS, we meet so many people. You're out there having fun and you just don't care. You don't have inhibitions. And there's no pressure. But when you're home, you see the same people in the same bars at the same singles joints. It's harder to break down the wall and approach people.

> —ANONYMOUS
> ST. PETERSBURG, FLORIDA

• • • • • • • •

I MADE THE MISTAKE OF GOING TO A MEETING of Parents Without Partners. I was a single mom. I met lots of nice men, but they were all emotionally wounded, with a child who was sad and/or traumatized. Avoid Parents Without Partners; you'll just end up with other people's baggage!

> —M.R.
> VALLEJO, CALIFORNIA

• • • • • • • •

IN GENERAL, I GO TO JEWISH SINGLES EVENTS with the mindset of going to meet friends, not to meet a guy. I usually go to singles events that are more group-oriented rather than dating- oriented. You can usually tell by who's organizing the event and where it's located whether it's going to be fun and more about hanging out or whether it's going to be more dating-oriented.

> —SARAH
> ATLANTA, GEORGIA

JUST ONE LOOK

I FELL IN LOVE AT FIRST SIGHT and we both consider each other soul mates. It is an amazing feeling—one of complete understanding and connection. All it took was our eyes locking onto each other and we were absolutely joined.

> —*ELIZABETH ZEDZIAN*
> *WHEATON, ILLINOIS*

OH YES, I BELIEVE IN LOVE AT FIRST SIGHT. I think the thing about love at first sight is that you don't always recognize it as love. I can look back to the first time I met my boyfriend and know now that there was an instantaneous bond.

> —*SARAH*
> *SEATTLE, WASHINGTON*

I'VE NEVER EXPERIENCED LOVE AT FIRST SIGHT. I'm sure it exists, anything's possible, but I'm pretty sure it's a very rare occurrence.

> —*DANNY GALLAGHER*
> *HENDERSON, TEXAS*

I BELIEVE IN LUST OR ATTRACTION AT FIRST SIGHT. Love—real love—requires time, trials, empathy and shared experience. I used to believe in soul mates—I don't know if I do anymore. I'm not sure if this makes me sadder or wiser, because I'd like to believe in soul mates. It just seems that so many relationships are based on mutual insecurity. Can you name more than a handful of couples who genuinely seem to be in love?

> —*LITSA DREMOUSIS*
> *SEATTLE, WASHINGTON*

Ignition Keys: Pickup Lines, Blind Dates, Perusing the Personals

Y*ou see an attractive person, or you read about someone great. Now what? From pickup lines to passive-aggressive profiles, here are thoughts on moving toward that first conversation.*

DON'T BE SHY. INTRODUCE YOURSELF. If I see a girl across the bar, I don't know what I'm going to say. I walk over and start off with a simple, "Hi, how are you. My name is so-and-so."

—*TONY MAIN*
LANCASTER, PENNSYLVANIA

PICKUP LINES ARE JUST A FUNNY WAY TO START A CONVERSATION.

—*JUSTINE MOJICA*
ATLANTA, GEORGIA

I WENT OUT WITH A GUY ON A BLIND DATE, and we were sitting at the bar talking. The bartender kept jumping into the conversation, as bartenders do. But I really thought I had so much more in common with the bartender, and I found myself flirting with him instead, while I was on this date with somebody else! At the end of the date, the guy I was with said goodbye and left the bar, but I stayed on alone and ended up talking with the bartender. And I ended up dating the bartender.

> —*KAMMY T.*
> *SAN FRANCISCO, CALIFORNIA*

If I want to talk to someone, I'll look at him and smile. If he doesn't come over, there's nothing else I can do.

—*KAYZE*
BALTIMORE,
MARYLAND

• • • • • • • •

DON'T OVERLOOK ONLINE PERSONALS, or a newspaper's classified sections. Don't be too proud to use these tools, because they allow you to bypass singles scenes and bars, and they don't put you at the mercy of your friends. I was too embarrassed to do personals for a while, then I tried it and met the most amazing woman I've ever known. And she was absolutely drop-dead gorgeous.

> —*M.T.*
> *CHICAGO, ILLINOIS*

• • • • • • • •

PICKUP LINES ABSOLUTELY TURN ME OFF. I think a guy should be original and spontaneous. If you can't do that, you're not the kind of guy I want to be hanging out with anyway.

> —*A.W.*
> *SWAINSBORO, GEORGIA*

• • • • • • • •

JUST BE APPROACHABLE. Opening lines never work—that's the problem. Opening lines are for suckers. I stay away from that.

> —*RYAN SIEVEKING*
> *ATHENS, GEORGIA*

I THINK PEOPLE ONLY USE ACTUAL PICKUP LINES in the movies. The real business of conversations starting between strangers is usually a slow, boring, predictable ritual, and not worthy of an audience.

> —*SHAUNA MCKENNA*
> *ST. PAUL, MINNESOTA*

• • • • • • • •

66**Blind dates are like Cracker Jacks. You never know what you're going to get!** 99

> —*D.T.*
> *SAN FRANCISCO, CALIFORNIA*

• • • • • • • •

IF SOMEONE CATCHES YOUR EYE, don't be afraid to go talk to him. Most of the guys that are worth talking to are not the ones that will approach you right away, ready to pounce with a cheesy pickup line. The worthwhile guys—the keepers—stand back from the crowd.

> —*JENNIFER D.*
> *PARK CITY, UTAH*

• • • • • • • •

ALWAYS HAVE STOCK THINGS YOU CAN TALK ABOUT —this is critical in bar situations. I'm not going to bring up my secret ones but you can ask something like, "Who's your favorite Muppet?" That's one that everyone can talk about. Or, "What celebrity do you look like?"

> —*E.R.*
> *ATLANTA, GEORGIA*

The most exciting period of dating is the beginning. Is he going to call? Are we going to have fun? What's going to happen next?

> —*RAY*
> *ROCKY MOUNT,*
> *NORTH CAROLINA*

I'M NOT THE KIND OF PERSON WHO USES pickup lines. I can't even remember jokes, so how could I possibly remember a line? Besides, someone who would fall for a pickup line isn't for me.

—*PHIL S.*
SAN FRANCISCO, CALIFORNIA

· · · · · · · · ·

GROANERS, BUT GOOD

ONE TIME I BORROWED MY BROTHER'S MUSTANG CONVERTIBLE and drove through the bank drive-through window where this pretty teller worked. I didn't even have an account with this bank, but when she asked me what transaction I would like to make, I said I would like to make a withdrawal and deposit. I would like to withdraw her from her office and deposit her at the movie theater with me. It worked!

—*JONATHAN ADAMS*
SAN FRANCISCO, CALIFORNIA

· · · · · · · · ·

THE BEST PICKUP LINE I USE INVOLVES A WATCH. I have this big, blue watch I wear out to the bars and when I start talking to a girl she usually comments on my watch. I tell her it's magic and she asks, "How's it magic?" And I say that it can tell what color underwear she's wearing, which usually prompts her to say, "Oh yeah ... what color are they?" And I reply, "You aren't wearing any." And she usually smiles and says, "Yes, I am." Then, I tap my watch, put it to my ear, and say, "Damn, it must be an hour fast."

—*D.A.*
CHICAGO, ILLINOIS

NO PICKUP LINE NEEDED: If you're a girl and you see a guy you like at a bar, simply stare. Then, walk over to him. Keep looking at him without saying anything. He'll be forced to say something to you first.

—*I.N.*
PATTON, PENNSYLVANIA

• • • • • • • •

FIRST GO FOR EYE CONTACT WITH A WOMAN. If you get it, go up and talk to her. Just say, "Hi. How are you doing? Are you having fun tonight?" If she was looking at you, too, she wants to talk so sparking a conversation shouldn't be too difficult.

—*MIKE*
STRAFFORD, NEW HAMPSHIRE

• • • • • • • •

I ONCE BOUGHT A GUY A DRINK. The guy came over and sat with me for a while and we talked. It worked well. I'm not good at walking up to people and starting conversations. So if I'm going to make the first move, I do something less direct, like buying a drink.

—*BARBARA*
OMAHA, NEBRASKA

• • • • • • • •

TRICK HIM. I make him think he's making the move. I find someone I'm interested in and who I want to ask me out. I flirt mercilessly. I go to group events with that person and completely focus on him. Finally, he'll ask me out.

—*ALLIE R.*
WASHINGTON, D.C.

Don't send a woman a drink: You're being a wuss if you do. You're saying that you can't go up and talk to her. Be brave: walk up and introduce yourself.

—*ANONYMOUS*
CLARK A.B.,
PHILIPPINES

COMPLIMENT PEOPLE. If I see someone who's well dressed, I'll try to compliment them—unless, of course, I'm not looking good that day. If you're wearing cutoff jeans and a Philadelphia 76ers shirt and you see someone and say, "Those are great shoes," it's probably not going to work for you.

—*D.S.*
    SAN ANTONIO, TEXAS

· · · · · · · ·

❝You just have to be confident and calm when you're on blind dates, even if that's not how you feel.❞

—*E.R.*
    ATLANTA, GEORGIA

· · · · · · · ·

A GOOD WAY TO ATTRACT MEN: Be a *Star Wars* fan. Know the dialogue for the first three movies. Guys are stupid about *Star Wars*. If you coyly "confess" to them that you really like The Original Trilogy, they will immediately turn into gooby teenagers and will think you are the most fun girl ever. Warning: Be prepared to field questions about the Princess Leia Iron Bikini. Once I lied to a guy and told him I had worn that outfit in a previous "adventure." He was putty in my hands from there on.

—*LISA*
    MINNEAPOLIS, MINNESOTA

BLIND LUCK: SET-UPS THAT TOOK OFF

GIVE IT A CHANCE. My friend practically had to drag me to her house that night. I kicked and screamed the whole way. I was still kind of involved with an old flame at the time, but my friend insisted that she had the perfect guy for me. I wasn't swept off my feet after our first date. I thought he was a nice guy, but I didn't see anything happening past that. I gave him a chance, and that's all it took. We were engaged in six months and married within a year.

    —M.J.F.
      WICHITA, KANSAS

LET YOUR FRIENDS SET YOU UP on blind dates. They know you, and sometimes they have a sixth sense about what sort of person you could be compatible with. A friend of mine set me up with my future husband after going on a blind date with him herself. She called me the next day and told me that she wanted to give him my number and something in her voice told me to go along with her plan. Normally, I wouldn't have agreed to go out with a complete stranger, but my friend insisted that he was a quality guy and she was right. We hit it off immediately.

    —NICOLE LESSIN
      HELOTES, TEXAS

IF YOU MUST USE A LINE...

A GUY HAS A SUGAR PACKET, and he gives it to you and says, "You dropped your name tag."

> —*CHRISTA*
> *CASTLE ROCK, COLORADO*

• • • • • • • • •

SOMEONE WALKED BY MY FRIEND and me and left a piece of paper on our table. It said, "Thank you for being beautiful." That's great. It made me smile.

> —*AMY*
> *MARIETTA, GEORGIA*

• • • • • • • • •

"HOW ABOUT BREAKFAST? Want to call me or nudge me?"

> —*A.R.T.*
> *SAN FRANCISCO, CALIFORNIA*

• • • • • • • • •

"YOU MUST USE WINDEX ON YOUR PANTS, because I can see myself in them."

> —*NICOLE*
> *CASTLE ROCK, COLORADO*

• • • • • • • • •

THE MOST EFFECTIVE LINE I EVER USED was the most honest one: "You have the most beautiful smile, and I really wanted to meet you."

> —*PAUL W.*
> *MINNEAPOLIS, MINNESOTA*

BE CONFIDENT AND DON'T BE AFRAID to talk to people. The way I do it is, I try to ask random questions like "Would you rather be a lobster or sea cucumber?" That's a test to see how willing a woman is to have fun. If she plays along, I know she might be fun to talk to. If she gives me a strange look, then I know I don't want to hang out with her.

—*ANONYMOUS*
BELLEVUE, WASHINGTON

You have to look for signs of interest. If a woman is not looking at you or not giving you any signals, don't hit on her. Women put out signals; You have to look for them.

—*RAY*
ROCKY MOUNT,
NORTH CAROLINA

PEOPLE DON'T GO OUT BY THEMSELVES, so the problem is infiltrating a group. If you've got friends with you, you can go up to a group of girls and start a conversation. But if it's just you, there's no one to back you up. One way to make a connection is to add a woman's drink order onto yours, or help her if she is having trouble getting the bartender's attention.

—*SCOTT C.*
LOS ANGELES, CALIFORNIA

THINK ABOUT IF THE SETTER-UPPERS really know you. It's often some random connection. They think, "Oh, they both live in Los Angeles—that should work."

—*N.D.*
SAN FRANCISCO, CALIFORNIA

NEVER, EVER ALLOW YOUR FRIENDS to set you up on a date because if the relationship goes sour, they can end up in the middle of the mess.

—*STEPHANIE B.*
NEW YORK, NEW YORK

I do blind dates regularly. They're always awful.

—*DEANNA ABNEY*
SAN FRANCISCO,
CALIFORNIA

I CAN'T TELL YOU HOW MANY TIMES I TRIED to smoothly pick up some hot babe at a club. But I can tell you that it's the exact same number as the number of times I failed. Turns out, I dance like the biggest dork out there. If you're going to make a move, first make sure you know how to move.

—*JERRY B.*
NEW YORK, NEW YORK

• • • • • • • •

WARNING: WHEN A GIRL SAYS THE FRIEND that she wants to set you up with is 'voluptuous,' that means "wide-body."

—*RICHARD*
ATLANTA, GEORGIA

DITCH AND DANCE

My current boyfriend rescued me from a terrible blind date. My best friend had set me up with her boyfriend's co-worker. We had nothing in common; the conversation was awkward and he kept talking about the past. A few hours later and a few drinks too many, I noticed this guy checking me out at the bar. I whispered into my date's ear that I was going to the ladies' room while nodding at the other guy. When I came out of the bathroom the guy from the bar was waiting for me. I quickly introduced myself and explained that I was on the worst blind date. We agreed to pretend to be old high school friends and I introduced him to my date. He played along so well that my date immediately bought us all a round of drinks. Then, I turned to the new guy and said "Hey, I remember that you used to be a great dancer back in the day," and I asked him to dance. He happily agreed and we went off on the dance floor and ditched my date. We've been together ever since.

—*V.B.*
NEW YORK, NEW YORK

BLIND, BOUND, AND GAGGING

My mom set me up with one of her friend's sons when I was in high school. He was cute in a Farmer-Brown-meets-Tom-Cruise sort of way. He had a funky little cowpoke accent which set off my city-girl alarms, but I decided to go with it. After about 45 minutes I asked him what he did for a living. He then proceeded to explain to me the art of bashing in a pig's head: He worked at a pig-slaughtering farm. He talked for at least 30 minutes about how just days earlier he had been knee deep in pig blood, feces, and remains. I had been a die-hard vegetarian for four years. Needless to say, our first date was our last. To this day I still think that my mom set me up with that guy in order to cure me of my crazy vegetarian ways. I never went on a blind date again.

—*Lee W.*

WHEN GOING ON A BLIND DATE, a liberal amount of alcohol helps ease the jitters. Whether you drink it before, during, or after the date is up to you.

—*Mia Kirchmeier*
Redmond, Washington

• • • • • • • •

I ENCOURAGE ANYONE WHO GOES ON A BLIND DATE to Google their potential mate before meeting. You'd be amazed at the things you'll learn.

—*Sarah Clark*
New York, New York

☆

In my romantic days, I once approached a girl at the mall and asked her, "What exactly makes your heart beat?"

—*Slim Clippins*
San Diego, California

IF YOU'RE INTIMIDATED BY BLIND DATES, ask your friends to invite you and the blind date to a more natural group activity, like a BBQ or volleyball game. One of my best set-ups was a group outing to a baseball game. We both knew we were there to meet each other, but it seemed like a much more low-pressure setting.

—*A.L.*
BOSTON, MASSACHUSETTS

• • • • • • • •

I WENT ON A BLIND DATE WHEN I WAS A NAÏVE teenager. He drove up in a Pinto, wearing a print polyester shirt unbuttoned to show off his hairy chest and several gold chains. After oysters— because he said they were a sexy food—he took me to a friend's house where the couple wanted to sleep with me. Fortunately, they paid attention when I said "no" and he took me home. The "friend" who set me up on this date thought it was really funny.

—*J.A.*
DURHAM, NORTH CAROLINA

• • • • • • • •

The wingman is not just there to get his friend to hook up with a girl; he's there to keep his friend from hooking up with the wrong girl. That is the true wingman.

—*KEITH*
MIAMI, FLORIDA

KNOW YOUR ESCAPE ROUTE. Last year I was set up on my first blind date and I didn't know a thing about this guy, so I asked my sister and her husband to go to the same restaurant and eat a few tables away from us just in case. My sister and I had a "code" signal—I would make eye contact with her and tug my earring if things weren't going well. She would then call my cell phone and tell me I had to go because my friend from out of town is at the house wanting to visit me. Fortunately for me, our system worked when the date took a bad turn!

—*JENNIFER W.*
IOWA

SOUND LIKE FUN?

D on't set up a date based on the sound of someone's voice. While working in New York, I had to speak daily with a receptionist at the printer. She had a sexy London accent and was very nice and flirty on the phone. When she mentioned she was going to be in my neighborhood one night, I volunteered that I lived nearby and we should meet in person and get to know each other. We decided to meet at a bookstore—a nice public place. We had never seen each other, so we described what we would be wearing. Upon arrival, I looked in the window, and my date was not exactly attractive. I decided I didn't care, as she was really nice on the phone, and I have no room to be so shallow. I should have left then. We went to a nearby restaurant for dinner, and things got worse as I got to know her better. She explained that she mainly dated police officers and gun enthusiasts that she met on the web, and most shared her love of the Confederacy. As things progressed, I realized she was borderline racist, right wing, and the opposite of anything I'd be interested in. She, however, thought the date was going smashingly, and I had to spend the next month avoiding potential second dates.

—B.N.
ATLANTA, GEORGIA

DON'T SAY IT

MSN.com picked what its editors believe are the 10 worst pickup lines. Number One on the list was, "What's your sign?"

DON'T GO SOMEPLACE ULTRA-FANCY for a blind date. It's overkill, and seems kind of desperate, I think. The best blind date I ever went on was when this guy took me out to a casual pizza-and-beer place—not tacky, but casual and fun. It made me relaxed, and we ended up hitting it off really well.

—*J.D.*
BALTIMORE, MARYLAND

• • • • • • • •

WHEN TELLING SOMEONE I'M NOT INTERESTED, I usually take the polite approach and make up an excuse about how I'm already seeing somebody else, I'm moving out of town, or I'm getting treated for an unusually troublesome case of gangrene. Some people are more blunt, and that works, too.

—*JESSE AMMERMAN*
LOS ANGELES, CALIFORNIA

Love at First Site: Internet Dating

From dating Web sites to Instant Messenger, e-mail, and emoticons, technology has transformed the dating world. Some people like to browse profiles; others like to keep it digital while they flirt. And everyone follows a certain etiquette. How does e-mail become "we-mail"? Read on to see what makes people "click."

THESE DAYS, IT'S NOT, "WHY ARE YOU doing online dating?" It's, "Why aren't you?" I have several friends that have gotten married to people they met through online dating sites. They are all ages, all kinds of people.

—*JULIE*
SAN FRANCISCO, CALIFORNIA

NEVER UNDERESTIMATE THE IMPORTANCE OF A SUBJECT LINE.

—*JEFF WILDER*
WASHINGTON, D.C.

THE INTERNET, IN GENERAL, AND E-MAILING, in particular, have been the most revolutionary dating developments. I would be lost without the ability to woo online. The e-mail flirtation, the exchange of words and images, the mingling of souls through correspondence, the sexiness of the suspenseful, delayed, or super-quick response—I owe at least the last three years of nooky to the Internet. Plus, if able, you can cyber-serenade the object of your affection by recording songs and sending them along. The wonder of it all!

—*LEE*
BROOKLYN, NEW YORK

Use e-mail to see how someone thinks. Some men I've met are great and write really well, but quite a lot of them are bad spellers, bad typists, or just morons!

—*L.G.K.*
EASTON,
PENNSYLVANIA

• • • • • • • •

INSTANT MESSENGER IS AWESOME because it allows you to say things you normally might not say in person. You can be a little flirtier, and, as weird as this may sound, those little smiley faces can really hint at a lot of things!

—*ALLY WEINSTOCK*
CHICAGO, ILLINOIS

• • • • • • • •

IF SHE GIVES YOU HER E-MAIL, you might as well e-mail her—but keep it short. It's like getting a phone number. Wait until she e-mails you back so you don't seem so desperate. But if she never does, go ahead and look desperate, and e-mail her again.

—*LEANG LIM*
EL CAJON, CALIFORNIA

• • • • • • • •

I LOVE E-MAIL RELATIONSHIPS. You can be cynical and funny and you get a hint of the true character of a person in e-mail. It's something you don't get with a phone call.

—*LISA*
NORTH CAROLINA

U R HOT. LETZ D8.

Dating in the United States is different than in England. There, it's all about that text messaging. I'll be talking to someone and they'll be glancing between me and their phone, nodding at me and typing into their cell. It's just accepted. And if you want to date, you'd better know how to text a girl. It's a good, casual way to flirt, to ask her out for a casual date. If you don't know how to text, you have a disadvantage against other guys who do.

—ANONYMOUS
LONDON, ENGLAND

* * * * * * * * *

Back when I was going to college, I met this girl on the computer while using a UNIX chat program. After we had been chatting awhile, we decided to meet in the computer lab. Anyway, I think I'm going to be clever and from the girl's description of herself I thought that this one girl was her. So I started coming on to her— you know, saying, "Hey, where would you like to go?" And before I really realized it, I started thinking, "What the hell—this girl's being a complete bitch towards me. She doesn't like me." It turned out to be the wrong girl. That was really embarrassing, because this girl thought I was a complete lunatic.

—JEFF
FOREST HILL, MARYLAND

I like to use e-mail to follow up on dates; it's much less stressful. You can just send an e-mail and say, "Hey, I had a good time."

—*JON WILLIAMS*
  CHICAGO, ILLINOIS

IF MY FRIENDS KNEW HIM and he wasn't a major scuzzball, I would probably give him my phone number. If he were kind of shady, I would give him my e-mail; very shady, a fake e-mail.

—*LIZ*
  ATLANTA, GEORGIA

• • • • • • • •

WHEN YOU'RE SEPARATED BY A LONG DISTANCE, e-mail is really the only way to communicate. One of the advantages of communicating by e-mail—instead of by phone—is that there isn't that awkwardness. There isn't that dead silence when you don't have anything to say. It also gives you something to look forward to. It's a good communication tool, and it definitely helps build friendships.

—*TERI BURNS*
  SYRACUSE, NEW YORK

• • • • • • • •

I WOULDN'T GIVE SOMEONE MY E-MAIL address unless I've been dating them for a while. I only e-mail my close friends. I like talking on phones better because you can hear tone of voice and tell if you like a person.

—*AMBERLY COY*
  SAN DIEGO, CALIFORNIA

• • • • • • • •

I DON'T LIKE INSTANT MESSAGING. A guy can put you on his buddy list and know every time you're online. It's like they're cyber-stalking you. That's not cool.

—*AMY*
  ATLANTA, GEORGIA

ONE THING I HAVE LEARNED ABOUT IM and text messaging is that it is a convenient, easy way to say hello; however, it is a terrible form of meaningful communication. My fiancé and I know now not to chat about anything that is serious or important. IM is fine for small talk ("How's work?" "What's on TV or the radio?"), but we don't chat about things that can become emotionally charged. Technology, leaves too much room with the lack of tone for misinterpretation. Most of all, it is a lot easier to be mean to a machine than it is to a person. In the heat of emotions, it is too easy to send something you will regret.

> —*ZAK CERNOCH*
> *SAN ANTONIO, TEXAS*

I DATED THIS GUY AND HE ALWAYS text messaged me and I hated it. I felt like it was a timid way of trying to talk to me, like he didn't want to call me. I prefer it if the guy actually calls.

> —*PEGGY*
> *ST. PETERSBURG, FLORIDA*

• • • • • • • •

ONLINE DATING IS ALL ABOUT VOLUME. It's like dating people in a crowded room. You might hit it off with two out of 50 people. Don't get discouraged. Look at it this way: It's a great way to meet new people. Some of them will become friends or lovers. Others will turn into great stories to share with your friends.

> —*D.R.*
> *ATLANTA, GEORGIA*

For a quick confidence boost during a dating drought, peruse the online dating databases to see just how many single people there are out there like you!

> —*COURTNEY*
> *NEW YORK,*
> *NEW YORK*

DATING SITES: PROS AND CONS

THE INTERNET IS AN UNBELIEVABLE AND, I might venture, revolutionary factor in modern dating. More and more people are identifying themselves with communities based not on proximity, but common tastes and interests. If you "know" dozens of people online who share your sense of humor, your taste in books and movies, your chosen lifestyle, why would you settle for someone who in person is smart but dull, nice but obsessed with dorky TV, and ten times less handsome than the people you've seen only in carefully selected snapshots? I think this is wonderful in some ways, because people can find their soul mates online. But it can be terrible in many other ways—namely, the new laziness in cultivating real-life relationships.

—*BETTE CRAWFORD*
PHILADELPHIA, PENNSYLVANIA

THE INTERNET CAN DRASTICALLY IMPROVE YOUR SOCIAL CALENDAR. Evite not only invites you to a party; you'll know ahead of time who's coming and who's not. Friendster introduces you to people you know through friends and friends of friends. E-mail gives your friends and dates one more way to contact you in case your cell phone dies. You always know what's going on, what the weather is going to be, and how to get where you're going. If you meet someone interesting, you can always Google their name and find out all kinds of stuff.

—*HALEY*
ATLANTA, GEORGIA

WITH E-MAIL, IM, AND CELL PHONES, it's much easier to get hold of people. There's no more waiting around for phone calls. This is good if you want to hear from somebody, but disastrous if you're trying to avoid her. She can track you down when and where she pleases, at all times. Guys have been forced to become more innovative with their excuses.

> —JESSE AMMERMAN
> LOS ANGELES, CALIFORNIA

* * * * * * * *

IT'S KIND OF NICE BEING ABLE TO SEND SOMETHING to someone's in-box and wait for an answer without having a long silence on the phone or face-to-face awkwardness. The Internet has made me less shy about showing my feelings. I've learned to be as open, blunt, and aggressive offline as I am online, and now it pays off.

> —JENNIFER STURM
> IOWA CITY, IOWA

* * * * * * * *

AS IN ALL THINGS, BE YOURSELF IN E-MAIL. Yes, brevity is a safe bet, but do you really want to be dating someone who doesn't appreciate your jokes about wandering carp salesmen? I don't think you do. Treat e-mail like a real-life conversation that gives you the added bonus of editing before you speak. And if you're not ready to make a date, end your e-mail with some nice conversational questions about the other person.

> —BETTE CRAWFORD
> PHILADELPHIA, PENNSYLVANIA

Picking the right photo to post can be hard if you are a woman. You want to find the one where your hair is just right and you don't look fat.

> —JAN JOHNSON
> VIRGINIA BEACH,
> VIRGINIA

I like e-mail. You can be really forward on e-mail. You can say, "You're really hot. When can we go out?"

—*ROBYN*
    ATLANTA, GEORGIA

DON'T ENGAGE IN OVERTYPING IN E-MAIL. You shouldn't respond with a novel to a one-sentence note. If you're going to be verbose, you can ask some questions and see if they put any time/thought into their response. Then, you respond accordingly.

—*EVAN*
    ATLANTA, GEORGIA

• • • • • • • •

I STARTED USING INTERNET DATING SITES about a year ago as a way to meet people. I think what made it work for me was that I wasn't really attached to any particular outcome. It was more about realizing I was ready and that I was committed to putting myself in as many situations as possible to meet the right guy. I made it a game and had fun with it. I figured the worst-case scenario would be that I would make some interesting friends and learn something about myself along the way. It turned out I met a real keeper.

—*T.L.C.*
    ATLANTA, GEORGIA

• • • • • • • •

WHEN I FIRST MEET SOMEONE, I never give them my e-mail address. When e-mail is involved, there are different expectations: so much is read into how you write, how much you write, and how soon you respond. It's not a good thing for the beginning of a relationship. I don't e-mail someone until many months into it.

—*SETH*
    NEW ORLEANS, LOUISIANA

WHAT I SAY?

Iwas e-mailing my friend and forgot to put the "1" after his name in the address. Some guy e-mailed me back and said that I had the wrong address. I sent a note back and thanked him. After that, we just started e-mailing. He lived in England and played in a band and worked at the *Financial Times*.

He was great. He didn't even compare to the guys I was seeing. It was awesome; I raced to my work to read his responses. It was the highlight of each day. But then I told him an innocuous little story about getting stood up for a date. And I think he decided from the story that I wasn't good looking. His replies started getting shorter. All of a sudden, it just stopped. We had e-mailed so much, for months. I couldn't ask him what was wrong. It wasn't that kind of situation.

> —LAURA
> BOSTON, MASSACHUSETTS

MAKE SURE YOU GET what you've been promised. I met this guy online and helped him with the Web site for his company that made bags, even before I met him. So, he told me he'd give me a bag when we met. Then we met, and it just didn't work out. I thought we would at least be friends, but he said he didn't want to be just friends. But I asked him for the bag anyway, and I got it! I never talk to him, but I use the bag all the time.

> —K.C.
> SAN FRANCISCO, CALIFORNIA

I only look at profiles that have pictures, but I refuse to put up my own. I don't want people to know I am doing it. I guess it's just me being self-ish.

—*Anonymous
San Antonio,
Texas*

I WOULD ASK A GIRL FOR HER E-MAIL before I'd ask for her phone number. If I wanted to make it completely obvious that I wanted to ask her out, then I would want her phone number. But if I was just interested in a girl and wanted to keep it ambiguous, I would go for her e-mail.

—*Jon Williams
Chicago, Illinois*

• • • • • • • •

I MET MY WIFE ONLINE, AT A DATING SITE. She found me and then wrote to me, not because I was the best-looking guy on the site but because we seemed to have a lot in common. I was the first guy she'd ever met through the dating site! I guess it's like dating in the "real world"; you need to go beyond looks to find true love. If you search for the right traits you'll find the real thing sooner.

—*J.R.
Chicago, Illinois*

• • • • • • • •

I LEARNED THAT YOU HAVE TO BE MORE CAREFUL about the subtext when you're meeting someone online. It's hard to know what words or e-mails really mean over the Internet. Things are a bit more obvious when it's person-to-person.

—*Laura
Boston, Massachusetts*

• • • • • • • •

I MET A GUY ONLINE and it was so nerve-wracking, meeting up for the first time after we'd done all that e-mailing and calling. I didn't want to get my hopes up and be disappointed, but of course I was hoping that there would be that physical attraction, that spark. It turned out fantastic, despite all my nervousness, and we've been married for over four years now and have two kids.

—*Rachel B.
Philadelphia, Pennsylvania*

MY PARTNER AND I MET THROUGH THE MAGIC of AOL. We spent a month chatting online, and after our first date in person we knew it was a match. The fun with AOL was just jumping out there and saying hello. It's kind of like fishing—you get lots of little fish before you find the big one. We tell people we met online and sometimes they are taken aback. But we think that in this day and age it's like meeting someone at a bar or a party. It's normal.

—*JEREMY CALEB JOHNSON*
VIRGINIA BEACH, VIRGINIA

E-mail works to break the ice and Instant Messenger saves on your long-distance bill.

—*M.S.*
DAVENPORT, IOWA

" **Don't lie about yourself in your profile; all it does is waste time for both of us.** "

—*N. CLARK*
HOUSTON, TEXAS

INTERNET DATING IS FUN, but realize that it's a fantasy world. When I was dating someone on the Internet, I could be whoever I wanted. So could he. Then I met someone that I really began to like. Luckily, we were both being truthful with each other. But we could have easily been deceiving the other person. I wasn't very careful, but it turned out OK.

—*ALICE*
POLAND

A TALL TALE

Never take for granted what someone states online about his or her appearance. I agreed to meet an online date at an upscale, trendy restaurant. She was already waiting at our table when I arrived. I was impressed that she had actually arrived a bit early. She looked just like the picture that she had sent to me through e-mail. We enjoyed a pleasant conversation throughout dinner. We were there for about two hours, and neither of us got up from the table the entire time. After I paid the bill, we stood up: she was a good half-foot taller than I was! She was obviously taller than the 5' 7" that she had stated online, and, to accentuate her height even more, she was wearing three-inch heels. She was gorgeous, and I felt that we had sort of clicked, but nothing hurts a guy's ego more than looking straight up at a woman. There was nothing that I could do, other than try to step back from her a bit so that our height difference wouldn't appear as obvious. I could tell that she, herself, felt a bit uncomfortable, but she didn't say anything. Upon walking out of the restaurant, I hinted at exchanging phone numbers, but she just sort of blew off the idea. We exchanged e-mail a couple of times afterward, but we never saw each other again.

—*T.G.*
DEARBORN HEIGHTS, MICHIGAN

YOU GET TO MEET SO MANY PEOPLE with online dating. When I was doing it, it was kind of exciting to come home and find ten new e-mails. My married friends were living vicariously through me. I would print out a profile and they'd say, "Oh, he's a good one!" or, "Yuck!"

—*HEIDI*
CHICAGO, ILLINOIS

• • • • • • • •

SOME ONLINE DATING SERVICES GIVE YOU the choice of sending a prospective date an e-mail or a pre-canned "tease." I normally don't respond to the teases. I find them a cop-out. My philosophy is, go big or go home!

—*ANONYMOUS*

• • • • • • • •

I SEARCHED THE PROFILES FOR COMMON INTERESTS. The things that were important to me were an interest in languages, travel, and some international experience. You have to see what they've rated as important to them and really think about what's important to you. A lot of the people talked about how much money they made, or that they were really religious, and those were turn-offs to me.

—*SIOBHAN FLEMING*
SAN FRANCISCO, CALIFORNIA

We met in person exactly three years after meeting on the Internet. Biggest surprise: He was taller than I expected!

—*AIDA S.*
NEW ORLEANS, LOUISIANA

• • • • • • • •

THE MAN I SEE MYSELF WITH ISN'T the kind of guy who would take time out of his life to painstakingly put together a fake profile on the Internet in order to meet the girl of his dreams. He would have more initiative than that.

—*AMBER*
RIDGEWOOD, NEW JERSEY

✓ **IT WASN'T SO IMPORTANT TO ME** that somebody's profile was catchy or clever. It was more important to me to look at the traits they had marked off. In fact, you really have to watch out for that—to not be enticed by a catchy paragraph. In my case, I was looking for somebody who talked about their kids and marked off that they didn't mind having more. I wanted someone who had a great relationship with their kids, because I had to know they could be a good stepfather to mine.

—*HEIDI*
CHICAGO, ILLINOIS

DATING DATA

Forty million Americans log on to Internet personals sites each month.

. . . .

DON'T TRY TO DESCRIBE YOUR SOUL MATE in your profile. You want to sound casual, fun, and funny, if you can. No one wants something super-deep. You're just looking at the profile to know if someone has the same interests and might be attractive. After that, you just have to figure it out for yourself. Trying to describe your soul and your soul mate is silly. It's never going to happen that way.

—*ANONYMOUS*
ATHERTON, CALIFORNIA

. . . .

WHEN READING PROFILES, go with your instinct. There is no trick to decoding it; it's a combination of what and how they write. Do they seem sincere? Do we have things in common? Do they sound educated? You need to consider these things. But on the other hand, you also have to keep an open mind because sometimes a good person will not necessarily jump off the page.

—*ELLIS*
SEATTLE, WASHINGTON

ALWAYS POST CURRENT COLOR PHOTOS. Your date will immediately know if you've posted an old or inaccurate photo. I had dates where the person looked ten years older than in the photo. One photo should be a close-up of your face. Another should be a full-body view. The others should show off your personality. Avoid including pets— it makes you look cheesy and desperate for love.

> —D.R.
> ATLANTA, GEORGIA

. . . .

I MET MY FIANCEÉ WHEN SHE CONTACTED ME. She wasn't registered on the site but she saw my profile and sent me an e-mail. It turns out, she has a similar corporate background; we're both executives in multinational companies. This appealed to me. We continued to correspond and we ended up meeting, after three or four weeks. The rest is history.

> —ANONYMOUS
> WESTON, FLORIDA

. . . .

DON'T GIVE UP ON IT. I had several dates with men I met online and most of them were losers! I came home and told my mom that I'd never do it again. But I saw my future husband's picture and started talking to him. I'm glad I gave it one more shot.

> —JANICE JOHNSON
> VIRGINIA BEACH, VIRGINIA

If you make contact with enough people through the Web, it can really help you hone your criteria and crystallize what you are looking for in a person.

> —C.M.
> CHARLOTTESVILLE, VIRGINIA

ON THE ENDANGERED LIST?

According to a study of 1,000 college women, dating is a dated concept at schools across the country. Either people hook up casually or settle in for an ultra-serious relationship.

I SKIM MEN'S PROFILES FOR ANY RED FLAGS, like, "I like women who are open-minded and like to have a good time." To me, this means he wants to find an easy lay with a tongue ring or something. There are plenty of those "read-between-the-lines" things. If he says, "I like independent women" or "50-50 relation-ships," I read, "Prepare to pay for your half of dinner."

—*ANONYMOUS*
NEW YORK, NEW YORK

• • • • • • • •

WHEN YOU'RE MEETING SO MANY PEOPLE online, don't give out your number too easily, even when you reach the phone-call stage. For safety and common sense reasons, I had the guys I wanted to date give me their numbers, and then I called them. The online dating services filter your e-mails, too, and don't give out your real address, so you can cut off some-body when you want to and not get all sorts of crazy e-mails. It's impor-tant that you don't get so enthusiastic and hopeful that you start acting unsafe.

—*RACHEL B.*
PHILADELPHIA, PENNSYLVANIA

• • • • • • • •

DON'T EXPECT TO MEET THE PERSON in the profile. I once read an online profile that sounded great—someone I'd really like to meet—and then I real-ized that I had met him before. He was far from how he portrayed himself online. People have a self-image that's possibly different from what they project to others.

—*ANONYMOUS*
SAN FRANCISCO, CALIFORNIA

THIS IS MY BEST SIDE

Have someone of the opposite sex look at your online profile. What guys think is great, women think is not essential, or inappropriate, or not critical to finding the right woman. I was involved in online dating, but I wasn't particularly active. While visiting a friend in New York, she asked me how the dating scene was going. I said, "Not so well." She looked at my profile and said, "This sucks."

She revised it and asked me to put up different pictures. I put a surfing shot out there and a picture of me on a dinghy in Laos— I was going to get someone who liked travel and liked to rough it a bit, as opposed to those would want to go to the Ritz Carlton. Also, I wasn't smiling in one of the previous pictures. Smiling is a good thing. As soon as I updated my profile, I got a hit from the woman who has been my girlfriend for a year.

Get someone to edit your profile for you. It's like writing an essay.

—DON REIGROD
SAN FRANCISCO, CALIFORNIA

WORDS OF WARNING

WHEN YOU ARE MEETING SOMEONE FROM THE INTERNET or from a personals ad, make sure you meet in a public place and make sure you have a lot of information and background on that person. Also, tell a friend where you are going to be and keep your cell phone with you. Recently, I had a friend who was date-raped by a man she met online via a personals ad. She met him in a public place and thought he was a nice guy. Unfortunately, she didn't have a lot of information about him. You can never be too careful or too safe.

> —*THERESE POPE*
> *SACRAMENTO, CALIFORNIA*

WATCH OUT FOR WEB SITES. They are full of men who only want to have sex, who just got divorced, or who are separating from their wives.

> —*DEONA HOUFF*
> *MOUNT SIDNEY, VIRGINIA*

I FIND THE INTERNET SITES A BIG RISK because you don't know who you are getting. I tried an online dating service, paid $1,700, and was totally scammed. It was a horrible experience. People I met were not serious about marriage; it was surprising. I also stay away from video dating services that say they are premium. The quality is no better than on the Internet sites.

> —*L.N.*
> *PEAR RIVER, NEW YORK*

YOU HAVE TO HOLD ON TILL YOU GET ONE that's really right. I went out on about ten Match.com dates before dating the man that I eventually married. Of course, a couple of them were crazy and strange, but most were pretty good guys. They were fun to see a movie with or just hang out with.

—*ELLIS*
SEATTLE, WASHINGTON

MAKE SURE SHE REALLY WANTS TO SEE YOU before you fly to meet her. I came all the way from England to see a girl from Alabama I met on the Internet. Unfortunately, by the time I arrived she had met someone else and didn't really want anything to do with me once I got there.

—*PAUL SMITH*
HALIFAX, WEST
YORKSHIRE, ENGLAND

FACE-TO-FACE APPROACHES are more intimidating, but at least they're real. In the online world there's too strong a temptation to tell yourself you're taking action to meet someone when you're really just paging through ads. You can be smart about it and not weigh it down with too many expectations, but there's still the danger of treating it as a substitute for trying to meet people in person.

—*CHAD MAKAIO ZICHTERMAN*
SAN FRANCISCO, CALIFORNIA

NET GAIN

According to an Elle Magazine/ MSNBC survey of online daters, 44 percent of women and 33 percent of men say they're getting more dates, more sex, and more lasting love as a result of using online personals.

I MET THE GUY I'VE BEEN DATING for the past nine months online. I had been through a string of bad online dates, but this guy was different. He was creative and funny; that's what caught my attention when we talked on the phone. Our first date was at a pizza place and he was charming, and didn't talk too much about himself (the kiss of death). I could tell this guy was interested in me, though. Soon we were dating three or four times a week. That was the best part—getting to know a complete stranger. It's always full of surprises—good ones and bad ones. That process of opening up to someone takes a while. It was probably about six months before we both felt completely comfortable with each other. Now I feel like I've known him for years.

—*D.R.*
ATLANTA, GEORGIA

• • • • • • • •

BE OPEN TO DATING SITES LIKE eHARMONY, where you don't have to share your picture. I met my husband this way. We were able to find out that we both liked the same music and shared common interests.

—*ANONYMOUS*
MERRICK, NEW YORK

• • • • • • • •

DON'T ASSUME THAT PEOPLE ACTUALLY READ your profile: many just look at the picture. Even though I listed myself as a liberal, I'm a magnet for Republicans. I even changed it to "very liberal" and it only got worse.

—*ANONYMOUS*
SAN ANTONIO, TEXAS

I-DATING ADVICE FROM A PRO

I've been dating people online for more than five years. The best metaphor I can use to describe the process by which you can meet people who are best suited for you: Approach online dating as you would a job search.

You wouldn't send in a generic resume, saying that you're a nice person who likes to work with people and is looking for a fun job, would you? Then why would you post a profile on an online dating service saying pretty much that? An attractive girl gets more than a hundred e-mails per week. You need to stand out!

Write your essays as you would your resume, highlighting the most interesting, attractive things about yourself. Instead of saying something like, "I like music," try, "I was raised on Led Zeppelin, Pink Floyd, and The Beatles, so forgive me if I'm not quite the urban hipster. I can, however, play guitar and can cover pretty much any pop song prior to 1990. And yes, I do take requests."

—EVAN MARC KATZ*
LOS ANGELES, CALIFORNIA

*(see credits page 207)

ON BALANCE, AN ADVANTAGE

I've exchanged emails with women I've met at various places—in fact, I had extended early-relationship contact via email with the current girl I'm dating.

The advantages:

1) Lower risk. It's much easier to take some time and write a clever email (or response) than it is to talk to a stranger on the phone.

2) More time. You can be very precise about what you want to say and how you say it.

3) Self-consciousness is less of a problem.

The disadvantages:

All of the above. If you can be charming from the ether, but not in person, you're in trouble.

    —EVAN
      ATLANTA, GEORGIA

First Dates: Taking the Plunge

*N*ow comes the hard part. You have to sit down with someone *you don't really know yet, make conversation, and then secretly decide whether this is someone you ever want to see again. Is there anything more awkward? To make it easier to take that first jump without getting soaked, we've asked hundreds of people about their first-date process. So before you get ready for your big date, read on.*

IT'S ALL ABOUT THE BUTTERFLIES. There's no better feeling than having that excitement in your stomach the first time you meet or kiss or anticipate seeing him again.

—*SARA C.*
REDDING, CALIFORNIA

DON'T BE PUT OFF BY THINGS THAT CAN BE CHANGED, LIKE CLOTHES.

—*HELEN KURTZ*
MINNEAPOLIS, MINNESOTA

The wacky dates are fun. I went out with a guy once and our first date was to the Bronx Zoo. It was a Saturday, it was fun, and it was different.

—*Justine Mojica*
Atlanta, Georgia

ADVICE TO GUYS ON THE FIRST DATE: Don't be late. Smell good. Dress nice, but casually. The first date is easy, simple. You're trying to get to know her. You don't want to be uncomfortable on a first date.

—*Tony Main*
Lancaster, Pennsylvania

• • • • • • • •

WHAT TO WEAR: IF IT'S UNCOMFORTABLE, he'll love it. If it's not painful, it just won't turn him on. Think high heels. Push-up bras. Thong underwear (you know; gluteus floss). And, God forbid, a Brazilian. Never show up for a date wearing sensible shoes.

—*Cindy Pfeffer*
Forest Hill, Maryland

"Guys think differently than girls. Girls are picturing us at the altar and four kids and a white picket fence. And we're just thinking about getting through the date and what we might do later. We're thinking about what she looks like naked."

—*J.S.*
Atlanta, Georgia

DEODORANT (CHECK), PANTIES (CHECK), GUM (CHECK) ...

When going on a date, I usually check three things before the evening even starts—I put on extra deodorant, I wear some cute panties, and I make sure that I have enough gum to share. Why are these so important? The first one is obvious. Nothing kills a date like smelly armpits. And I sweat a lot, so I pack on extra deodorant to make sure that my overly active pores don't ruin the date of a lifetime with an extremely wonderful man. The cute panties, well that's just Murphy's Law. The minute I opt for the comfortable white cotton, granny panties, the guy I'm hot for wants to get hot with me. And when he sees those bloomers, it's a major turnoff, *not* like in "Bridget Jones Diary." And lastly, the importance of gum. Well, nothing else kills a blissful moment like cigarette breath, garlic breath or any breath that isn't minty fresh.

—VIRGINIA
LOUISVILLE, KENTUCKY

The best place to go on a date is a place where you can eat. Food is a good conversation starter.

—J.A.B.
SAN FRANCISCO,
CALIFORNIA

SOME WOMEN'S MAGAZINES HAVE REGIMENS for preparing for your date—an hour-by-hour countdown ranging from morning yoga ("so you're flexible on your big night!"), to getting a facial, manicure or some body treatment, to "shopping with a girlfriend for a last-minute date accessory… a bracelet or scarf," to a whole make-up walkthrough. I find this funny and pretty offensive, too. I hardly want to spend my whole Saturday "prepping for that special night"—too much effort reeks of desperation.

—ANONYMOUS
AUBURN, CALIFORNIA

• • • • • • • •

GO SOMEWHERE NEITHER OF YOU HAVE EVER BEEN before; it can be a good bonding experience. My former boyfriend and I had both always wanted to go water skiing but had never done it. We tried it on our fourth or fifth date, and we had a blast. With something new you both get to learn together and nobody goes into the date with an advantage.

—ERIN DELEONIBUS
PITTSBURGH, PENNSYLVANIA

• • • • • • • •

DON'T GO OUT FOR A DRINK and force conversation. Instead, do an activity together like bowling, hiking or rollerblading. That way, you'll learn more about them and have something in common to talk about.

—B.N.
MINNEAPOLIS, MINNESOTA

DO SOMETHING DIFFERENT; try a kid-oriented activity (go to the Science Museum, or go play at Lego Land). My personal favorite is to go to Toys R Us and walk up and down the aisles playing with all the "sample" stuff. And if they don't have samples of the coolest toys, open up the boxes and make your own samples. It can be hours of fun.

—*J.S.*
EDINA, MINNESOTA

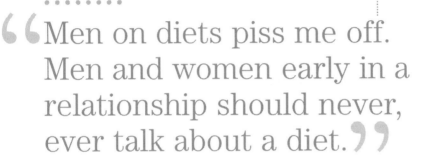

"Men on diets piss me off. Men and women early in a relationship should never, ever talk about a diet."

—*P.J.*
NEW YORK, NEW YORK

PLAY POOL OR GO TO THE BOWLING ALLEY, something where there's an activity involved, to see how the guy reacts in different situations. Also, you can get the competitiveness going. I love competitiveness. You can egg one another on and you get the true spirit of someone.

—*LISA*
NORTH CAROLINA

NEVER MAKE DATE NUMBER ONE a dinner date. You don't know this person, so spending $80 is ridiculous. It's not even about "impressing her." First dates should be about conversation over a drink.

—*KEN K.*
SAN FRANCISCO, CALIFORNIA

When meeting someone in person for the first time, have high hopes, get your nerve up, and take the plunge.

—*RACHEL B.*
PHILADELPHIA, PENNSYLVANIA

DON'T TAKE ME SOMEPLACE REALLY EXPENSIVE on a first date. I'll feel uncomfortable. I'll feel like I owe you something and if I don't like you that much then I feel bad. It's a waste of your money.

—AMY
ATLANTA, GEORGIA

Any first date that involves ice cream is generally a good sign.

—N.S.
CITRUS HEIGHTS,
CALIFORNIA

• • • • • • • •

ON A FIRST DATE BE YOURSELF, if you're likeable. If you're not likeable, hopefully you know it and you can pretend to be. If you're not likeable but you can get through six months pretending you are, then you can convince anyone that the real you is likeable and the person you seem to be is the result of stress, from family, work—it might even be *her* fault.

—M.P.
MIAMI, FLORIDA

• • • • • • • •

FIRST-DATE RULES

When I go on a date, I'm always big on the manners thing. Open her door; they notice that stuff. Never talk about previous relationships or conquests. Don't complain about ex-girlfriends. Be in the moment and be positive, not negative. Definitely look them in the eye, even if they're not the greatest thing you've seen. If you've got the wandering eye, they're going to freak out. Also, you definitely want to go somewhere that doesn't have pictures of the food on the menu. And you need to have a plan if you ask someone out. But once your portion of the date is over, it's OK to give her the option to be in control. They want that anyway. And don't make a plan for the next date on that current date. Let it settle for a while. You don't want to come on too strong.

—J.S.
ATLANTA, GEORGIA

JUST BE YOURSELF ON THE FIRST DATE. You probably have something in common with the girl. You've just got to find that common ground.

> —*TRAVIS WIDNER*
> *ATLANTA, GEORGIA*

• • • • • • • •

I WENT TO AN NBA GAME FOR A FIRST DATE a little while ago. It was super fun because the game was exciting, so we could talk about the game while we were having a getting-to-know-each-other chat. And there was that mystery, because we would only make occasional eye contact.

> —*T.J.*
> *GRASS VALLEY, CALIFORNIA*

• • • • • • • •

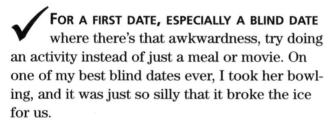 **FOR A FIRST DATE, ESPECIALLY A BLIND DATE** where there's that awkwardness, try doing an activity instead of just a meal or movie. On one of my best blind dates ever, I took her bowling, and it was just so silly that it broke the ice for us.

> —*M.S.*
> *NEW YORK, NEW YORK*

• • • • • • • •

OPEN DOORS FOR WOMEN. Walk on the street side of the sidewalk. Be respectful to waiters and valets and anyone else you encounter on a date. Make eye contact. Eat slowly. Don't litter. I once sat among a group of female friends as they discussed a date one of them had been on the night before. Women notice everything. And they interpret everything, many times over.

> —*HANK*
> *SAN FRANCISCO, CALIFORNIA*

Make fun of other people. That gets the conversation going. It takes the spotlight off you and puts it on other people.

—*MIKE*
  ATLANTA, GEORGIA

STAY CONFIDENT AND HAPPY ON A DATE. No matter what you are wearing, you will look more lovely if you smile. Poutiness is not attractive!

    —*ELOISE MILLIKEN*
     CALIFON, NEW JERSEY

• • • • • • • •

IT SOUNDS ROMANTIC AND CHEESY, but I would love it if someone were to bring me flowers at the start of a date. And then I'd like to go to dinner and have some drinks. For me, having drinks helps me loosen up and get to know people better. And I love driving. I would love to drive around the city, cruising, looking at the lights and neighborhoods.

    —*ANNE*
     WILMINGTON, NORTH CAROLINA

• • • • • • • •

❝There is something about a man cooking dinner for a date.❞

   —*L.G.*
    ATLANTA, GEORGIA

• • • • • • • •

 THERE IS NEVER AN EXCUSE for not practicing good manners, and if you think that a woman won't notice, then you're fooling yourself. Be a gentleman and take care of her needs without prompting: open doors, pull out her chair, never walk ahead of her, offer your coat when she's cold.

    —*P.W.*
     HARRISONBURG, VIRGINIA

PATIENCE, A SENSE OF HUMOR, and, of course, "the rescue call" from the best friend. If you're going on a first date and don't know whether you're going to want to escape after the first drink, it's always a good idea to have a friend call your cell phone with a made-up mini-crisis to give you a way out.

—*ILONA WILLIAMSON*
NEW YORK, NEW YORK

• • • • • • • •

BE PREPARED. If someone has planned the evening, it impresses me. Dinner and a movie are fine, but if somebody buys a ticket in advance or gets advice from a friend about a place, it shows he cares. On one date, this guy took me to out to eat and said at one point, "Oh, yeah, I dropped by earlier and looked at the menu and you might try this …" It was just kind of sweet.

—*ANONYMOUS*
BOSTON, MASSACHUSETTS

• • • • • • • •

TAKE THE PLUNGE AND ASK HER to dinner rather than just coffee. Asking a woman out for coffee gives one of two impressions: You are too cheap to pay for dinner, or you are unwilling to take the time.

—*WENDIE KAREL*
CHANDLER, ARIZONA

• • • • • • • •

DO SOMETHING COMPLETELY DIFFERENT on a first date. One of the best dates I ever went on was when I took a girl to a children's storytelling session at a library. It was a great date. It was not what she expected to happen, and it was fun.

—*STEVEN GROSS*
MANCHESTER, GEORGIA

If you're on a first date, watch how much you drink. Catch a buzz, fine. But you're trying to find out who this person is. If you're drunk that makes it difficult.

—*JOHN PIRIO*
NEW ORLEANS,
LOUISIANA

FOR A FIRST DATE, GET A DRINK in a comfortable hotel bar or something with couches or big comfy chairs and mood lighting. Bars and barstools are so un-sexy and very "stiff." People feel more at ease in the comfy setting.

—*ANONYMOUS*
NEW YORK, NEW YORK

• • • • • • • •

ON MY FIRST DATE WITH ONE WOMAN, I wanted to stand out in the crowd. So I took her to salsa dancing lessons. I was a bit uncomfortable with that kind of dancing, but she was pretty good at it, and I just tried to have fun. It must have impressed her because she went out with me again.

—*TONY T.*
SAN FRANCISCO, CALIFORNIA

• • • • • • • •

ON A FIRST DATE, MAKE IT A DOUBLE DATE and go some place public. It takes the pressure off so you don't feel like you always have to break those awkward silences. It also helps when something goes wrong. For example, my first date with my future wife was a double date with a couple I had known for some time. We went to a restaurant for dinner. Halfway through the dinner, I started feeling sick. Because it was a double date, the other couple covered for me, keeping my date entertained, while I was hurling in the restroom.

—*DAVID*
SYRACUSE, NEW YORK

• • • • • • • •

MY FAVORITE DATES ARE SIMPLE ONES that let us get out in nature. My idea of heaven: Two people in a hammock in Maui.

—*TAMI W.*
SAN FRANCISCO, CALIFORNIA

INVEST IN THE FIRST DATE. Before you meet the woman, go down every side street of your neighborhood and try cheap, random restaurants that no one else would know. You'll look like a culinary expert who's plugged into the city and knows about interesting places.

> —*JEFF WILDER*
> *WASHINGTON, D.C.*

Don't ever take a first date out for ribs.

—*MIKE*
DENTON, TEXAS

LIGHTS, CAMERA... ACTION?

THERE'S A THEORY THAT MOVIES MAKE BAD FIRST DATES. Sure, it's an anti-social meeting—you're in the dark and you can't talk to this person sitting next to you whom you've just met. Debunking that myth, I have had good movie first dates. If you've spoken to your date and there's been some banter, or maybe you had time to grab a drink beforehand and there's chemistry, a movie can be fun because it increases the intrigue. A nudge in the dark is sexy, romantic, and if you're able to laugh together, that's great. A movie might give you a sense of his/her humor radar. If it's an interesting movie, you'll have something to talk about at dinner—or at least on the way to dinner. I wouldn't pick just any movie, but if it has some depth, it could give you a good basis for conversation or insight.

> —*E.L.S.*
> *BERKELEY, CALIFORNIA*

DON'T GO TO THE MOVIES. The worst first dates of my life have all been movie dates. You don't get to know the person at all, it's unoriginal, and it can be really uncomfortable if there are any sex scenes. Avoid the movies and go somewhere you can talk!

> —*M.S.*
> *NEW YORK, NEW YORK*

TAKE TIME TO THINK ABOUT TOPICS you and your date can talk about. I picked topics that would be inspiring to my date and fun to talk about for both of us. If you go in prepared, it'll make her feel important and show that you really care about what interests her. I went out with a girl who was getting her master's in special education. So, I picked topics related to that.

—W.O.
SYRACUSE, NEW YORK

Don't forget to ask, "Why don't you tell me about yourself?" A lot of guys miss that question. They just talk and talk and the girls get bored.

—YONATAN ELKAYAM
LOS ANGELES,
CALIFORNIA

• • • • • • • • •

IF YOU'RE "JUST DATING," WHAT YOU NEED is someone who's a fun date. Find someone who likes to do the kind of things you like to do. Then just be happy that you get to go out and do things with somebody. Dating can be as simple or as complex as you make it. There's no need to think about every date as a potential marriage partner. Just go out and have a good time.

—L.

• • • • • • • • •

IT'S ALWAYS NICE WHEN A DATE FINDS OUT things about you before you go out and chooses something based on that, rather than just saying, "Let's go to dinner and a movie." I went to a sorority event that involved country swing dancing and had a great time. A guy I knew there noticed that. When we next saw each other, he mentioned that he was going to go country swing dancing and asked if I'd like to go with him.

—TAYLOR MCGINLEY
PULLMAN, WASHINGTON

THE WAY, SOME SAY

SUCH AN OLD CLICHÉ, BUT SO TRUE: The way to a man's heart is through his stomach. One time I made this killer meal for a new boyfriend, and he paid me the ultimate compliment: "I think this is even better than my mom could have made!" We dated for years.

—*MICHELLE*
SAN FRANCISCO, CALIFORNIA

I HAD JUST COMPLETED A 12-WEEK COOKING COURSE, and I love to cook, so I was excited to use some of my new abilities. A friend of a friend had introduced me to someone. We hadn't met yet but had two nice conversations, peppered with a bit of laughter, so we agreed to go to an art opening, and he was going to come over to my place first because I was truly excited to cook. So it was mostly about my experience, not so much about my date's. But there was no spark, except from the oven. So I had prepared this meal, yet the evening was flat. Lesson: Wait until you know someone better to have him over for dinner. There's too much "at steak!"

—*K.*
OAKLAND, CALIFORNIA

BOWLING OR SHOOTING POOL IS ALWAYS FUN on a date. Those are usually unplanned post-dinner activities, where if you had a good time at dinner, you choose something like that to continue hanging out together in low-key environment.

> — *B.*
> *SAN FRANCISCO, CALIFORNIA*

• • • • • • • •

 FOR A FIRST DATE, I LIKE TO GO OUT FOR A WALK in the country. I live in the country, and we'll just walk outside my house, follow the stream, walk the hills, and have a nice day out. You're taking in nice scenery as well as talking.

> —*PAUL SMITH*
> *HALIFAX, WEST YORKSHIRE, ENGLAND*

• • • • • • • •

KNOW YOUR AUDIENCE. I went out on a date with this guy who showed up in a hot red convertible sports car. He took me to some pretentious dinner and sent back the bottle of wine—not once, not twice, but three times. Maybe this would have impressed some women, but not me. I would have been so much happier with a beat-up old car and some beers and burritos.

> —*ANDREA*
> *BURLINGTON, VERMONT*

• • • • • • • •

 **IF YOU ARE TAKING SOMEBODY OUT** for the first time, find a place where you can have a conversation. Don't go to a movie. I had a date with a girl recently and we went into the North End of Boston but we didn't do anything elaborate. We went for a walk, we tried out the shops, we had coffee. It was just a good, casual date.

> —*JASON*
> *MYSTIC, CONNECTICUT*

FOR FIRST DATES, I'M A FAN of the daytime date. It's less contrived; you can wear comfortable clothes. And it's conducive to variety—you could walk from a museum to lunch to a park, which I call the hat trick. But honestly, it really doesn't matter what you do or where you are. A first date is more about spending the day laughing and having a great conversation.

—*R.*
OAKLAND, CALIFORNIA

• • • • • • • •

GET DOWN TONIGHT?

DON'T TRY TO MAJORLY HOOK UP on the first date: that's a bad move. Wait 'til the second date.

—*JAMIE*
PHILADELPHIA, PENNSYLVANIA

• • • • • • • •

I WENT OUT WITH A WOMAN ON A FIRST DATE, and things were going fine until I felt something tickling my leg. She had taken off her shoe and was rubbing her toe on my leg. Well, she miscalculated. Many guys might like that sort of thing, but I never called her again.

—*YEHUDA*
CAMDEN, NEW JERSEY

• • • • • • • •

I'D KISS A GUY AT THE END OF THE FIRST DATE. After that, it just depends on what I thought about him. Don't have sex if you think it will make him like you: That's something an 18-year-old girl would do. Don't do it if you don't feel like doing it.

—*KATE*
ATLANTA, GEORGIA

If a date did not go well, walk the woman home or to a cab, and say, "It was very nice to meet you. Take care." Nothing more, nothing less.

—*Jeff*
  New York,
  New York

PAY ATTENTION: IF SHE TALKS ABOUT HER ex-boyfriend at all during the first date, it means she is not over him. And believe me, life is too short to be constantly compared to a hard-bodied Olympic swimmer who "just didn't know how to commit."

—*Frank*
  Berkeley Heights, New Jersey

• • • • • • • •

THE WORST PLACE FOR A DATE is either a noisy place or the movies (you just met her and you can't talk for two hours?), or someplace where bad habits are revealed—like, if you had a gambling or betting problem and went to the racetrack or a casino.

—*H.P.*
  San Jose, California

• • • • • • • •

TRY A BREAKFAST/BRUNCH/LUNCH DATE, instead of an evening date. That way, you have easy escape routes built right in. My first date—a blind date—with my wife was for breakfast. Also, it's not too expensive. So I treated, which comes across as nice and chivalrous, and that helped me make a good impression on her.

—*J.W.*
  Rochester, New York

• • • • • • • •

ON THE FIRST DATE, NEVER TAKE HER to an expensive place. They'll expect it in the future and you end up spending a lot of money. On first dates, I don't take them to dinner. We usually have drinks. I'm kind of a cheap guy.

—*Tal*
  Washington, D.C.

TURN OFF THE CELL PHONE. I went on a date just recently with a guy who didn't turn his cell phone off and it kept ringing throughout the meal. It was just his friends checking in and he was like, "Hey, I'm out on a date. What are you doing?" I'm like, hello. Needless to say, we're didn't date after that.

—*AMBERLY COY*
 EL CAJON, CALIFORNIA

• • • • • • • •

IF SHE'S WEARING A "BORN AGAIN" PIN or some sort of really political pin when you pick her up, don't even bother with the date. You can imagine that she'll start pushing her religion or her politics on you pretty soon.

—*BAKER*
 ATLANTA, GEORGIA

CONVERSATION STARTERS FOR UNCOMFORTABLE SILENCES

"Have any pets?"

"Where did you get that _____?" (Ask about a specific piece of jewelry or clothing.)

"Have you ever _____?" (Ask about something that you are knowledgeable about or enjoy doing.)

"Do you like sports?"

"Have you ever been to _____?" (Ask if he or she has ever been to a local hotspot that you enjoy.)

(Brian Caniglia, DateSeeker.com)

COFFEE IS AS FAR AS I'LL GO on the first meeting; I want an out. There's no large investment of time or money. It's not too intimate so expectations are low. Besides, when you meet the right person, you know.

> —*DON REIGROD*
> *SAN FRANCISCO, CALIFORNIA*

• • • • • • • •

 WHILE YOU'RE TRYING TO GET TO KNOW someone, being punctual for the dates is imperative. It's a simple matter of respect. I've found that you can tell a lot about a person and how they feel about you by how closely they stick by the time that has been appointed.

> —*EILEEN MCCARTHY*
> *PITTSBURGH, PENNSYLVANIA*

• • • • • • • •

I LIKE TO GO TO A BAR ON A FIRST DATE. You can have a few drinks and get to know him. And if you don't like him, you can say, "I'm gonna go over here for a minute." And if you do like him, you can sit there and totally focus on him and you don't even realize what else is going on.

> —*CRYSTAL*
> *BREMEN, GEORGIA*

 • • • • • • • •

IF YOU'RE LOOKING FOR A LONG-TERM relationship, trust your instincts about him right off the bat. After your first date, what does your heart say? Could he be someone you could spend some serious time with? Don't try to kid yourself. Somewhere deep inside you will have a sense for people even after just one night out.

> —*COLLEEN JASTRZEBSKI*
> *BULGER, PENNSYLVANIA*

LOW-INTEREST DATING

I met a really nice-looking guy. He took me out to dinner, and all he did was talk about his job as a mortgage lender. And it wasn't because he was passionate about his occupation—he basically bitched about it the entire time.

Halfway through dinner, I think he realized he needed to stop talking so he could eat the food getting cold in front of him. So he asked me a question: "What's your current interest rate?"

I told him and he berated me for being a sucker and said that I was getting ripped off, and boy, could he fix me up with a better rate. So then the conversation turned from all-about-him to all-about-what-he-could-do-for-my-mortgage-rate. He took me home and invited himself in. I'm thinking, "Well, maybe we can make out on my couch. That'll shut him up." Oh, no.

As soon as we walked in my door he said, "OK, get out your W-2s from the last two years, your last two pay stubs and the original paperwork from your first mortgage." Then he put all my paperwork in a file and left. He called me the next day to tell me he could lower my interest rate by three percent. I came into his office, signed the papers, and never heard from him again. I wasn't sure if it was a date we were on or if that's how the guy solicits business. But it doesn't really matter: I didn't find a love interest, but I sure got a great deal on my mortgage payment.

—*Haley*
  Atlanta, Georgia

YOU DON'T ALWAYS HAVE TO BE POLITE. And you certainly don't have to sit through the rest of dinner if your date starts discussing his newly acquired "itch" before the appetizers arrive. Yes, it has happened to me; unfortunately, those uncomfortable moments turned into an entire night of discomfort because I didn't have the guts to excuse myself. Have some self-respect—don't crawl out the window. Just walk out the door.

—*COURTNEY*
NEW YORK, NEW YORK

* * * * * * * *

"Use the kiss test. On Date One, sometime during dinner, stare at her and ask yourself, "Do I want to kiss her?" If yes, keep going and see what happens. If no, it's bad news and get out A.S.A.P. "

—*AMOL DIXIT*
MINNEAPOLIS, MINNESOTA

* * * * * * * *

INVITE A GIRL ALONG TO AN ACTIVITY you do well, and then teach her how to do it, too. It's a great way to show off and also to get her involved in something you like. If you're lucky, she'll get into it and you won't have to make the choice between the activity and spending time with her.

—*S.M.P.*
PORTLAND, MAINE

HOW DO YOU GET OUT OF A BAD DATE once you're in it? Say, "I have to go to bed early. Thanks a lot. I had a really great time." And the next time he calls, say, "I just don't feel like there's any chemistry between us. I'm sorry. I don't want to waste your time."

—*DONNA*
  ATLANTA, GEORGIA

• • • • • • • •

I MET A GUY RECENTLY who told me where he worked, so I Googled his name. I saw his company profile and found out some personal information about him, like the sports he played in college. It was too forward for me, because when I went out with him and he introduced different conversations, I knew some of the background already. I felt like a stalker. Better to let things unfold naturally.

—*MARY*
  RENO, NEVADA

• • • • • • • •

ALL TOO OFTEN, WOMEN HAVE PRECONCEIVED notions about what a date is going to be. You think it's going to be perfect. You're getting ready, you're all excited, and you're thinking, this is going to be the best date I've ever had. But for whatever reason, he might not be as interesting as you want or as fun as you want, and you're ready to dismiss it. But you can never tell from a first date. There may be other things that went wrong. Who knows? The guy could've had a bad day or he could be nervous, and you're judging him on that. So, if you don't like the guy but you know he's a good person, you should always go on a second date to see what happens. Things may be different.

—*LISA*
  NORTH CAROLINA

DATING DATA

20,160: That's how many minutes the average person will spend kissing during their lives. That's 336 hours or 14 straight days of lip-locked bliss.

DON'T SHARE TOO MUCH ON THE FIRST DATE. I don't need to know that you're on Prozac. I don't need to know that you were in foster care. I don't need to know that your mother died when you were 14, or that your grandmother has Alzheimer's. Stick to shallow stuff on the first date. We can get deeper as the relationship goes on. Tell me about your job, where you're from, your hobbies, your interests. Talk about current events, the books you're reading, what movies you've seen lately, where you travel, where you want to go. These give me an indication of who you are.

—*ANONYMOUS*
CINCINNATI, OHIO

• • • • • • • •

ON THOSE REALLY BAD DATES, just keep reminding yourself that the night will eventually end and you will always come home at some point, put on your comfy cozies, and snuggle up in bed with a good romance book.

—*KRISTIN*
SEATTLE, WASHINGTON

6

Women: Read This!

D**o you want to know what guys really think? No? Well, maybe not, but be brave: the advice in this chapter from men (and some wise women, as well) can only improve your dating experience.**

A LOT OF GIRLS THINK IF YOU'RE NOT TALKING that you're not having a good time. That's what I hate—when I'm not saying anything and they keep asking me questions about what's wrong.

—*ALAN*
MEMPHIS, TENNESSEE

IF YOU'RE A GIRL DATING A GUY, DON'T NAME HIS MALE PART "PRINCESS SOPHIA."

—*JOE*
CASTLE ROCK, COLORADO

LOOKING FOR MR. EVERYTHING

Most of the women I know are always trying to find Mr. Right, but what they have in mind translates poorly from theory to reality. They're always looking for a man who's sensitive, spontaneous, and understanding, who anticipates every need, always knows the right thing to say, puts his girl-friend first, does thoughtful or romantic things without being prompted, keeps things clean and tidy, fixes broken things, cooks great meals... Come on now—most guys have full-time jobs already. Where are they going to find the time to be all those things for you?

Pick one quality that's important and just find a guy who's really good at that one. You know that you don't actually want to go on dates with Mr. Sensitive because he's so whiney and moody all the time. You can't plan a date with Mr. Spontaneity because he's busy flying by the seat of his pants. Is Mr. Need-Anticipator so desperate that he has nothing better to do than be there to go on dates with you all the time? These are just examples, but admit it ... they're not really important qualities when you're dating. Whereas, show-ing up on time might be an important quality if you're going to a movie that starts at a certain time.

—*ANONYMOUS*
  BELOIT, WISCONSIN

WOMEN ALWAYS THINK THEY NEED to be skinny to be pretty and get dates. I never liked really skinny girls. I like girls with curves, who look healthy, who can enjoy a good meal. No guy I know would actually prefer to date an anorexic, bony supermodel, no matter how good they look in magazine photos. We'd much rather be with normal, nice-looking, healthy, fun women. And I'm considered a good-looking guy. Women, don't be so stressed about your weight!

—*ANONYMOUS*
TUCSON, ARIZONA

MY GIRLFRIEND GOT ATTACHED VERY FAST. I mean, after two weeks she was talking about serious commitment. My advice for all the girls out there: Even if you are thinking it, don't say things like that so soon. It only freaks us out and makes us run for the door! Which is, by the way, exactly what I did.

—*BENNETT*
NEW YORK, NEW YORK

GIRLFRIENDS KNOW BEST

Want to know if your relationship will last? Ask your girlfriends. It seems the most accurate predictors of a romance's viability (even better than the couple themselves!) are a woman's friends. So, the next time you need a sounding board, dial 1-800-girlfriends.

Women who smoke—total turn-off. Beauty only goes so far when your clothes, hands and mouth are reminiscent of an ashtray.

—*G.*
  NEW YORK,
  NEW YORK

FIRST OF ALL, LISTEN. When he says that he has no intention of marrying because he is a confirmed bachelor, he means it. Nine out of ten times you will find it to be true. Don't take this as a challenge because you could win and spend the rest of your life trying to prove to him that he is happy!

> —*G.T.*
>   *PITTSBURGH, PENNSYLVANIA*

. . . .

I REFUSE TO GO OUT WITH A GIRL who's in her 30s. They think they're going to get married soon. I've seen it with a lot of friends of mine. They get the ultimatum. And at this point in my life, I can't deal with that. Girls should just go with the flow and see what happens. Girls, don't put a lot of pressure on guys.

> —*TAL*
>   *WASHINGTON, D.C.*

. . . .

I CAN'T STAND A WOMAN WHO is overly aggressive. I was in a relationship in college with a woman who was really attractive. It was the kind of fling where you don't care about anything but the looks. It only lasted for a few weeks; then she got bossy. Bossy and high-maintenance. Bossy and bitchy. I need a woman who is more soft-spoken. More feminine. When I told this woman I wanted to break it off, she couldn't believe it. It had never happened to her before, because she was so hot.

> —*JEREMY FORCÉ*
>   *BOSTON, MASSACHUSETTS*

10 WAYS TO IDENTIFY A LOSER

If your man has done any of the following, run:

1) If he asks for a beer at breakfast

2) If he has to call his mother before staying over

3) If everything he owns fits in one or two boxes

4) If he only drives a bicycle

5) If he used to have a drug problem, but now he has found God

6) If his last address included Department of Corrections

7) If he is married but it is just not working out

8) If, when describing him to your friends, you find yourself using the phrase, "But he's a really nice guy"

9) If he takes you to 7-Eleven for a chili cheese dog

10) If he asks to borrow money on the first date

—SHAWN M. GREEN
MELBOURNE, FLORIDA

DON'T BE AFRAID TO SPEAK UP and ask for what you want on a date. Don't just say "yes" all of the time. If you express your wishes, you'll have a much better chance of having them come true.

—*ELOISE MILLIKEN*
CALIFON, NEW JERSEY

• • • • • • • •

Don't buy a ticket to Egypt after you've only known a guy for two weeks.

—*KRISTIE DISALVO*
BOSTON,
MASSACHUSETTS

LADIES, BY THE THIRD DATE IT'S TIME for the baseball hat, sweats and no make-up! Then you will find out how he really feels. The real you needs to be seen very early. First impressions are important, but often aren't real. This goes for Internet dating, too. Put real pictures of yourself up on the site!

—*JANE DEBATTY*
DENVER, COLORADO

• • • • • • • •

THERE'S SOMETHING I CALL "husband-handsome." You don't want a guy who looks like he just stepped off a *GQ* page. He's just trouble. You have to worry about too many other women throwing themselves at him. And he's probably got an attitude. A guy who is just "husband-handsome" is fine, and ultimately, you'll be happy waking up with him thirty years from now.

—*DANIELA*
CORTE MADERA, CALIFORNIA

• • • • • • • •

I ALWAYS HAVE AN IQ TEST FOR WOMEN. I ask them how many senators can be elected in each state. Most young women don't know that answer, because it's not taught in schools nowadays, I guess. But if she doesn't get the correct answer to that, I'm done with her. There's nothing we can talk about.

—*TODD KASIK*
CHICAGO, ILLINOIS

SOME THINGS SHOULD BE LEFT UNSAID. I went on one date and the girl kept stopping me mid-conversation to tell me how great the date was going. Four times, she did that. It just was so strange because I didn't feel the same way. She said it was the best date she ever had and all this stuff. She kept saying, "This is going really well." I just never called her again. Don't say everything that's on your mind when you're on a date. You don't want to scare the guy.

—*J.S.*
ATLANTA, GEORGIA

• • • • • • • •

IF YOU'RE A GAL AND YOU GO ON A DATE with a fellow, don't act surprised when he tries to touch your skivvies. Really! Women act so surprised when you try to make a move on them. But men have been doing that for thousands of years; it's nothing new. It's just part of the dance. If you don't want it, tell us so. But don't be offended that we tried.

—*STEVE*
LONDON, ENGLAND

• • • • • • • •

Turnoffs: Smoking. Guns. Smoking guns. Any large animal weighing over 300 pounds, with big pointy teeth.

—*CHAD MAKAIO ZICHTERMAN SAN FRANCISCO, CALIFORNIA*

THAT COLOGNE IS SO... DIFFERENT

Women are likely to choose mates whose body odor differs from their own natural scents. According to theories proposed in a Swiss study, the collision of odors may somehow create better immune protection for their offspring.

The one thing I don't under-stand about girls is why—even though *they* don't know what they want—they still expect *you* to know what they want.

—*PETER FROST
CASTLE ROCK,
COLORADO*

MY ADVICE TO WOMEN IS TO NOT BUY anything for a man at Christmastime if you've only dated a month. I had been dating a man for about four to six weeks just before Christmas. It's hard to know what type of gift is appropriate, especially for women to give to men. I ended up buying a scarf—a nice one, but not overdone. I think he was appreciative, but in all honesty, if I had it to do over again, I wouldn't have bought him that. Instead, I would have made a nice dinner or done something instead of bought anything.

—*JENNIFER VERMILLION
NEW YORK, NEW YORK*

• • • • • • • •

I RELY ON THE "UNSTABLE CHROMOSOME" THEORY. Men have an X and a Y chromosome, while women have two Xs. The Y chromosome is missing a leg, which makes it unstable, which in turn makes men generally unbalanced. Reminding myself that it's not him, it's that damned unstable Y chromosome, helps me keep some humor in the situation.

—*DEBBIE
CHICAGO, ILLINOIS*

7 Men: Read This!

All we can say about this chapter is, a word to the wise (from the wise) ought to suffice. You really need to know the sage advice contained herein. Don't worry; you won't have to change.

SPEAK FROM THE HEART. What women appreciate more than anything is sincerity. You can give a compliment, but if you don't mean it, they'll see through it.

—*YONATAN ELKAYAM*
LOS ANGELES, CALIFORNIA

I CAN'T STAND THE SMELL OF SMOKING. EVEN IF HE DOESN'T SMOKE AROUND ME, IT'S ON HIS BODY, HAIR, CLOTHES. IT REEKS.

—*YVONA FAST*
LAKE CLEAR,
NEW YORK

> I like guys who have nice shoes. You can tell if the guy is a dork or not by the kind of shoes he wears.
>
> —*T.H.*
> *CHICO, CALIFORNIA*

YADDA YADDA

On average, a woman will speak 7,000 words over the course of a day while a man will only speak 2,000 words in the same time period.

DON'T LIE TO IMPRESS A GIRL. I went on a date with a guy who was obviously a pathological liar—I mean he even did the "I'm a secret agent" lie. I'm sure he thought I was naïve and gullible, but I wasn't impressed at all; I thought him ridiculous.

> —*JENNIFER W.*
> *IOWA*

* * * * * * * *

I'M DATING THIS GUY AND HE TEXT MESSAGES me during the day. He'll say something like, "Thank you for being a positive part of my life." It's like getting flowers. It brightens someone's day. And you don't have to buy anything. Some men think women want these grand acts of sacrifice, but it's the little things like that. We're not that hard to please.

> —*CINDY STEVENS*
> *SAN DIEGO, CALIFORNIA*

* * * * * * * *

MEN, DISPLAY GOOD TABLE MANNERS. One date from this past fall sticks out in my head, because my date ordered soup at dinner; it was a thick bisque. He dropped his spoon in the soup and then fished it out, licking the spoon handle, and he resumed using it. I was pretty grossed out. And to make it worse, the waiter from across the room noticed his spoon fiasco, and presented him with a new spoon. My date shook his head at the spoon offering, saying, "Thanks, but that's OK." I never thought basic table manners would make or break a date.

> —*D.V.*
> *MARYSVILLE, CALIFORNIA*

EVEN IF YOU DON'T KNOW IF IT'S A DATE, dress up nicely. I asked a girl to a movie once and she said yes. In my mind, I didn't think it was a date, but she took it as a date. So I didn't dress up; I wore old jeans. But she was dressed up nice—her nails polished, her hair sprayed, everything. We went on this date, but I pretty much killed it with my outfit. Sometimes I think about what would have happened if I had dressed up that night. You never know: We might have started dating, and then—who knows.

> —BIG J.
> TAIPEI, TAIWAN

I WORK AT THE FRONT DESK IN A DORM at the University of Iowa and my advice to guys is: You only need one squirt of cologne! People walk through the door doused in half a bottle.

> —LACEY I.
> IOWA CITY, IOWA

WOMEN AREN'T NECESSARILY LOOKING for someone to wine and dine them, but if you ask a girl out, at least pay for her on the first few dates. It would be nice to be treated like a "princess" in the beginning.

> —J.
> BOSTON, MASSACHUSETTS

ISN'T THERE A BOYFRIEND BOOT CAMP out there somewhere? Girls need a place to send their men. There are plenty of guys out there, but most of them could use a little work—like learning how to call us, show up on time, and to admit that supermodels wouldn't make good dating partners.

> —CINDY PFEFFER
> FOREST HILL, MARYLAND

Guys shouldn't talk just about themselves. Most men are very guilty of that. If I wind up being someone's therapist on a date, they never get a second date.

> —ANONYMOUS
> CINCINNATI, OHIO

E-CARDS AND INSTANT MESSAGES seem to have replaced flowers for apologies these days. On the one hand, I've found that guys are quicker to admit their wrongdoings now. But the apologies aren't as "quality" as they used to be.

—*LISA*
MINNEAPOLIS, MINNESOTA

• • • • • • • •

"Never, ever wear black sneakers on a date. Most women hate black sneakers!"

—*WENDIE KAREL*
CHANDLER, ARIZONA

• • • • • • • •

SURPRISES WORK WONDERS. Valentine's Day was always a fighting holiday for me and my boyfriend of five years, because he never got me anything. By year four, I got so sick of it that I bluntly told him he had to get me something because it was really embarrassing when people asked what I'd gotten and my answer was, "Nothing." So he did—a box of chocolates. Only, when he gave them to me, he was like, "I'm sorry they're unwrapped, but I already ate one." I was like, "What?!" I couldn't believe that he'd finally been thoughtful enough to buy me a present, yet he'd ruined the moment by eating one of the chocolates. That was when I opened the box and noticed, in the missing chocolate's place, he'd slipped a ring.

—*KATHARENE JOHNSON*
RIDGECREST, CALIFORNIA

HOW TO STEAL A GIRLFRIEND

STEP ONE: Tell the man she is going out with that you intend to steal her from him. Be prepared for a barrage of threats or even a physical confrontation. The other man will become paranoid and jealous. He will question her daily about her plans before letting her out of his sight. He will scrutinize her attire. ("Why are you wearing that revealing outfit just to go out with the girls?") He will drive her insane.

STEP TWO: Create the impression that you are seeing her when he is not around. Call her at home when he is there and have a casual conversation. If she laughs as she is talking to you, this will increase his jealousy and poor behavior. Be seen walking out of her place of business when he arrives to pick her up or visit her.

STEP THREE: Establish yourself as a sympathetic ear. As he becomes more clingy, make sure she turns to you to complain about his neurotic behavior.

STEP FOUR: Wait. Eventually, his insecurity will become unbearable and she will dump him. Then you can move in and ask her out.

—*DANIEL DUNKLE*
ROCKLAND, MAINE

I know for sure that I am not looking for a man who has long hair. If that moment ever comes, I'll rent an Antonio Banderas movie. A guy with a pony-tail is a total turn-off.

—*ANONYMOUS*
SAN FRANCISCO,
CALIFORNIA

ONE OF THE SEXIEST THINGS A BOYFRIEND ever did for me was serenade me. He was just a pretty good singer and an OK guitar player, but one night with the lights down low, he sang to me. My heart just melted. If you can sing at all, that is a sure way to a woman's heart!

—*SHANNON L.*
SAN RAFAEL, CALIFORNIA

• • • • • • • •

SURPRISE HER. I started seeing someone recently. I work from home, so one afternoon last week, the doorbell rings, which is normal because FedEx delivers a few times a week. But when I answered the door I had a surprise lunch delivery from a nearby café and potted flowers. From my guy! How sweet! It's a great feeling when you know someone is thinking about you. Unfortunately, when the doorbell rang this week, it was the UPS guy (who is cute, but not my type).

—*D.*
SAN JOSE, CALIFORNIA

• • • • • • • •

MEN, YOU SHOULD GO OUT OF YOUR WAY, find something that's special to your girlfriend, and surprise her with it. Once, my boyfriend wrote me a beautiful invitation for a date. He said the evening, which was my birthday, was going to be a surprise. We drove 90 minutes to my home-town and checked into a hotel. We had a very nice dinner and went for a walk around town. One of my favorite singers was playing at the local theater. Sure enough, he had gotten us great seats for the concert. It was the most romantic and best date I've ever had.

—*M. & M.*
KIRKLAND, WASHINGTON

NEVER UNDERESTIMATE THE POWER OF ROMANCE to win the girl. My husband and I started dating right at the end of the Colorado ski season. I had spent the season working in Colorado and had decided to move there from California permanently. So I left Colorado to go home to pack up my things. Every day for that month I got something in the mail from my boyfriend. He sent a pine bough, some snow—admittedly melted—in a Ziploc baggie, some dirt from the town where we live, and many, many postcards. It kept him in my mind while we were apart.

—*ANDREA COX*
GRAND LAKE, COLORADO

It's important for a guy to show genuine interest. Not just interest because you want to hook up, but because you really want to get to know her.

—*ALISON*
NORTHFIELD, MINNESOTA

TAKE OFF ALL CLOTHING while having sex. One time I looked down and saw he was still wearing socks—black, standard-issue socks—though nothing else. I don't know why it struck me as ridiculous, but it did.

—*BETTE CRAWFORD*
PHILADELPHIA, PENNSYLVANIA

✓ **A LOT OF GUYS THINK THAT THE WAY** into a girl's heart is to suck up to her through excessive compliments and gift-buying. Of course, giving too many compliments to a woman, especially about her looks, only makes you look needy and desperate. It gives her the green light to walk all over you. On the other hand, some guys have the philosophy that you should never compliment a woman. But this isn't right either. Giving a compliment can be very powerful with a woman when you say it directly, smoothly, and with no apologies.

—*P.W.*
HARRISONBURG, VIRGINIA

• • • • • • • •

❝Don't use a coupon for 20 percent off the meal on your first date. I was tempted to do that one time: I'm a real tightwad. But then I realized that was probably not a good idea.❞

—*TODD KASIK*
CHICAGO, ILLINOIS

• • • • • • • •

DON'T BE CHEAP. I once had a date use his student ID to buy tickets when he had been out of college for seven years. When I meet up with people like this, I usually just drink and try to get the night over as soon as possible.

—*E.B.*
ATLANTA, GEORGIA

ALL GUYS SHOULD KNOW THAT when you take a girlfriend to a family function, you shouldn't expect her to mingle with your family while you leave her alone. This has happened to me several times, but most recently, my ex-boyfriend took me to his sister's wedding and just left me sitting at the table with his aunts and uncles and I had nothing to say.

—*A.F.*
IOWA CITY, IOWA

• • • • • • • •

DON'T TALK ABOUT THE FOLLOWING THINGS, unless you know the woman and know she is also interested in the thing you're talking about: baseball, The Grateful Dead, former girlfriends, your mother, your car, your cell phone, golfing, and politics. What should you talk about? Her. Ask lots of questions about what she likes, about her job, about her family, about where she has traveled. The more she talks, the better you're doing.

—*M.J. TWETTEN*
CHICAGO, ILLINOIS

Never let your date catch you checking out another girl. If you have to crane your neck, chances are she's going to catch you.

—*ANONYMOUS*
ALEXANDRIA,
VIRGINIA

• • • • • • • •

YOUR BOYFRIEND SHOULD HAVE NICE relationships with your friends, even if just out of respect for you. When I first started dating my first boyfriend, he never wanted to hang out with any of my friends. He just refused to make the effort to get to know them, and at the time I was slightly annoyed but didn't think it was abnormal. So it was a big dilemma, having to always choose between him and my friends, and finally it was just too difficult. I lost many of my close friends in the process. Now, I realize that it doesn't have to be like that.

—*DACODA K.*
NEW YORK, NEW YORK

A GUY SHOULD NEVER CHECK OUT other women on a date. When I'm with someone, he should make it seem like I'm the most important thing. I hope I make that person feel that way, too.

—*CINDY STEVENS*
SAN DIEGO, CALIFORNIA

• • • • • • • •

"Don't talk about your ex-girlfriends. Girls don't like that. They're funny that way."

—*JIMBO-2*
ATLANTA, GEORGIA

If she wants to watch *Law and Order* (yes, I know it's the 27th night in a row), turn off the Cardinals game, suck it up, and smile.

—*SAM C.*
INDIANAPOLIS,
INDIANA

• • • • • • • •

NEVER TELL A WOMAN THAT SHE IS getting upset when you are in the situation of being yelled at. Never tell her that she is being irrational. Just shut up and listen. And when she is done, ask her if there is anything else—women will use ammunition from months ago against you.

—*DOMINIC STABILE*
FOREST HILL, MARYLAND

Rules: Made to be Broken (-Hearted)?

Sometimes the rules of the game are printed on a sign or pub-lished in a book. But in dating, most rules are invisible (especially when it comes to picking up the tab). If you don't know them, you risk ruining a great date. Then there are those who love to break the rules, and who still live happily ever after. Read on—you be the judge.

I DON'T LET ANYONE GET TOO CLOSE until I decide that I like his view of the world. To keep that distance, I maintain certain rules. For example, I won't let him visit my apartment or call me at work. And I definitely will not meet his parents! I'm surprised at how many men want me to meet their parents.

—CARMEN
OAKLAND, CALIFORNIA

MEN LIKE THE CHASE. THEY LIKE TO BE THE HUNTERS.
—MARK JAPPE
SANTEE, CALIFORNIA

Guys should always pay (or try to) because girls spend most of their money on clothes.

—*MARK FRANKLIN*
CASTLE ROCK,
COLORADO

IF YOU ASK SOMEONE OUT ON A DATE, you need to be the person who pays for the date, regardless of whether you are male or female. Women should offer to pay, even on the first date. Say something like, "Can I help you with that?" If the guy is worth his salt, he will never take you up on it (at least, not on the first date). But it gives the guy the impression that you're gracious.

—*WENDIE KAREL*
CHANDLER, ARIZONA

• • • • • • • •

I THINK THE PERSON WHO ASKS SHOULD PAY. They can also agree (in advance) to both pay for themselves, but it's important to know where you're going. I wouldn't hesitate to tell someone, "That's above my budget," if he suggested something that really was out of my range.

—*ALISON BLACKMAN DUNHAM*
BROOKLYN, NEW YORK

• • • • • • • •

❝The asker should pay on the first date. If the person who was asked out then pays, it seems like mooching. And if you pay equally, it feels more like a friendly outing than a date.❞

—*STEVEN GLASSMAN*
DELRAY BEACH, FLORIDA

I AM A FAN OF CHIVALRY AND OF GENTLEMEN who know how to treat a lady, but I think the question of who pays depends on the situation and the person. I have no qualms about paying for my dinner, but I do like to be treated, and I do enjoy a man spoiling me. Also, when you work in non-profit like I do, the rule of thumb is, "Don't look a gift horse in the mouth!"

> —*THERESE POPE*
> *SACRAMENTO, CALIFORNIA*

THE GUY SHOULD ALWAYS PAY on the first date. Guys who let you pay on the first date end up taking you for granted. Always. If there's ever any awkward feeling once the bill has been delivered—like he may think you should go halves—I just go to the restroom for a long time. It never fails. The bill is paid when I get back.

> —*LISA*
> *MINNEAPOLIS, MINNESOTA*

MY DAD SAID THE GUY should always pay. It's a form of encouragement. It's like saying, "You don't have to worry about anything. I have it under control. You just have a good time." If the girl wants to step in and help, that's cool, too.

> —*DOMINIQUE COLEMAN*
> *SYRACUSE, NEW YORK*

Chivalry is lost on me—I don't think the guy should be expected to pay. If he offers, fine, but I'm perfectly comfortable going Dutch.

> —*KRISTEN J. ELDE*
> *SEATTLE,*
> *WASHINGTON*

Always let the man pay. At least that way you won't be broke when he breaks your heart!

—*Erika Walker*
Seattle,
Washington

I WANT A PARTNERSHIP RELATIONSHIP so I like to start with shared payment. I can tell a lot about a fellow's real ability to accept adult equality by his acceptance of this. If I wanted to see him again I'd agree that whoever invited paid. I can tell a lot about someone by how they handle inviting, choosing a place and paying for dinner. I can also tell them a lot about my expectations by doing the same.

> —*Marilyn Barnicke Belleghem*
> *Burlington, Ontario, Canada*

· · · · · · · ·

A MAN HAS TO STEP UP TO THE PLATE and make the plans, lead the show. If they wimp out and I have to do it I'm so turned off. At least have a couple of options to show you have put some thought and creativity into it.

> —*Deanna Abney*
> *San Francisco, California*

· · · · · · · ·

❝Definitely the guy should pay. Chivalry will never die.❞

> —*Danny Gallagher*
> *Henderson, Texas*

· · · · · · · ·

IT'S BEEN SAID MANY TIMES BEFORE, but guys need to remember they should pay for the first date. Very often, women will attempt to split the check with you, but pay for the whole thing anyway. Very rarely, a woman will insist on splitting it, in which case, go ahead and do so. The idea is to show her some respect, and to demonstrate that you're no cheapskate.

> —*Steve Damon*
> *Manchester, Pennsylvania*

GIFTS: TOO MUCH TOO SOON—OR NOT ENOUGH?

IF YOU'RE DATING SOMEBODY CASUALLY, it's not such a good idea to give or get gifts. I think flowers are weird and cheesy. And anything expensive would not be OK. Jewelry cannot happen the first year or two of dating. I'd be a little weirded out if a guy I had been casually dating was like, "Hey, I got you these earrings."

> —C.C.
> *SEATTLE, WASHINGTON*

· · · · · · · ·

THE BEST GIFT I'VE EVER RECEIVED FROM A DATE was a teddy bear. It was really cute and I could keep it in bed with me. The worst gift was a penny that he found on the ground.

> —*EVA MCKENDRICK*
> *WINNETKA, ILLINOIS*

· · · · · · · ·

WHEN YOU GO SHOPPING, TRY TO REMEMBER THE THINGS your girl-friend likes and then surprise her. When we first started dating, my girlfriend told me she liked this dress and that she was going to save up and buy it. A week later I brought it home to her. She appreciated that. It's the little things.

> —*NICHOLAS AUSTIN*
> *ATHENS, GEORGIA*

· · · · · · · ·

I USED TO DATE THIS GUY WHO WAS REALLY INTO NATURE, so for his birthday I gave him a telescope, and for the holidays, I named a star after him.

> —*CARRIE K.*
> *CHICAGO, ILLINOIS*

It's kind of a requirement that the guy pays on the first date. It's respect.

—*JAMIE*
PHILADELPHIA,
PENNSYLVANIA

WHOEVER COMES UP WITH A GOOD PLAN for the second date sooner should call first. If the first date went well, then neither of you will be concerned about seeming too needy or eager. If you're already worried about whether or not you should call, then maybe you shouldn't be planning that second date.

—*SHAUNA MCKENNA*
ST. PAUL, MINNESOTA

• • • • • • • •

GUYS SHOULD MAKE THE PLANS ON A DATE. I hate it when a guy asks you out on a date and then asks you to choose what to do, because then you feel the pressure of not knowing what they want to spend.

—*PEGGY*
ST. PETERSBURG, FLORIDA

PENNY WISE, PLAIN FOOLISH

I went out with this guy once and we met at a small cafe. We had a great time, had dessert and tea and stuff like that. It was time to go and the waitress brought the check. He picked it up immediately, so of course I thought he would pay. After much studying and some silent methodical calculation, he turned to me and said, "Your half is $11.23." I was shocked! He went halves on me and down to the penny. So cheap, so rude. I was disgusted so I took the bill, put my Amex on top and settled it. I said to him, "I don't do halves." The moron had the nerve to try to kiss me after the end of the date and I gave him the cheek. I never returned his calls.

—*S.G.*
RALEIGH, NORTH CAROLINA

CALL ME ANYTIME?

DON'T CALL HIM! Men are so much more interested if you are somewhat aloof and seem too busy to call him.

> —*ERIKA WALKER*
> *SEATTLE, WASHINGTON*

• • • • • • • •

GUYS, CALL WITHIN A WEEK if you're interested.

> —*CRYSTAL*
> *BREMEN, GEORGIA*

• • • • • • • •

WAIT THREE DAYS BEFORE CALLING HER. If you call the next day you seem too eager. And if you wait a week, she might get a little pissed off. If you meet someone on a Friday or Saturday, then you can call on Tuesday or Wednesday to line up something for the weekend.

> —*MIKE*
> *ATLANTA, GEORGIA*

• • • • • • • •

HE SHOULD CALL FIRST. He'll say, "I had so much fun tonight. I would love to give you a call later this week. Does that work for you?" And then she can respond, "That's great, I look forward to it." Also, he should give it only a day or so. Not five days; that's absurd!

> —*ANONYMOUS*
> *NEW YORK, NEW YORK*

• • • • • • • •

EVERYBODY PRETENDS they don't have rules about calling, but everybody thinks, "Well, maybe I'll wait." If you want to call me the next day, call me. I'm not going to think we're married or freak out on you.

> —*KATE*
> *ATLANTA, GEORGIA*

The one who
asks the other
one out drives
and pays. It
avoids that
awkward
moment when
the check
comes.

—*Tary Paris*
Lincoln,
Nebraska

ALWAYS, ALWAYS OPEN THE DOOR for a girl on the first date. I don't care if your door is on the other side; you're going to have to walk around and open her door first. Do it. If a guy doesn't open a door on the first date, it can mean so many different things that lead into places you don't even want to venture.

        —*Stacey E.*
         Raleigh, North Carolina

IF YOU DATE LONG DISTANCE, make sure to see each other at least once a month, if it's financially possible. Don't let more than a month go by without actually seeing each other.

        —*Anonymous*
         Reading, Pennsylvania

A GUY HAS TO OPEN YOUR CAR DOOR for you. And they shouldn't honk the horn when they pick you up. And they should pay for the first date. After that, we are all professionals and we work. If I like a person and we get further into the dating, I offer to pay.

        —*S.A.F.*
         Tampa, Florida

GIRLS, IF A GUY TAKES THE TIME to send an e-mail to you saying he enjoyed last night, send a reply back. Don't just leave it hanging. And if you don't want to see him again, send an e-mail saying you're not interested. I can handle a cold e-mail; I've gotten a couple. I'd rather know than not hear back.

        —*Keith*
         Long Island, New York

SWITCHING ROLES ...

STAY AWAY FROM METROSEXUALS, and keep alert for the warning signs. I met this guy at a wedding. His mom was his date, and at the time, I thought, "Oh, that's so cute." He was dressed so nice and he was a lawyer. He invited me over to eat dinner and watch his favorite show—*Queer Eye For the Straight Guy*. His apartment was impeccable. He had two—*two*—dried silk flower arrangements. There was an elaborate sushi spiral and a tofu pyramid and Asian dipping sauces. He gave me a present—a candle that he had hand-wrapped very carefully. He talked about shopping, and he said something about his Armani shirt. That's weird, the whole thing. Girls don't need that.

　　—KRISTIN K.
　　　PHILADELPHIA, PENNSYLVANIA

• • • • • • • •

NEVER GET INVOLVED WITH A MAN who takes longer to get ready in the morning than you do! And beware of gay men in denial. If you get along as best friends, enjoy the same romantic comedies, shop together as a fabulous Friday-afternoon date, and never kiss, the man might be in denial. If your friends all thought he was gay and if strange men hit on him in the streets, trust their instincts. And if he tells you about the time he and his sisters dressed in tacky ball gowns and platform shoes as a joke for a family party, realize that your relationship was never meant to be—but don't be afraid to ask for fashion advice!

　　—HEATHER M.
　　　ALEXANDRIA, VIRGINIA

HE GOT THE POINT

GIFTS DON'T HAVE TO BE EXPENSIVE, but put some time and thought into it, people! When I was in college, I was dating this guy very seriously. We both went on separate spring breaks. I went with my family to Ireland and spent lots of time finding the perfect Irish cable sweater for him. It was beautiful and cost about $80. When I gave it to him, he said, "I got something for you, too," and he proceeded to give me a Fort Lauderdale pencil holder, which he clearly bought for $3.99 in the airport on his way back. I felt like I needed to teach him a lesson, so I put a little hole in it and wore it as a necklace. Of course, people kept asking me what I was wearing, and I told them, "Isn't it lovely? This is the present my boyfriend bought me." After that, he put more effort into getting me good gifts.

> —ANDREA
> BURLINGTON, VERMONT

. . . .

IT'S OK TO BE CORNY. On our one-year anniversary, my boyfriend and I were apart so I sent him a video date, where I had a friend follow me on a date to a restaurant, playground and beach. I even had him pick me up, where my parents pretended to interrogate him. Of course, the hardest part was keeping conversation going the whole time. I mean, I went on a date with a video camera—of course it was weird. But I mailed it to my boyfriend and he loved it. He thought it was sweet and he felt like he was actually there.

> —N.
> OXFORD, MISSISSIPPI

. . . .

ALWAYS BUY YOUR GIRLFRIEND something when you are away on a trip; everyone likes to know they were thought of from far away.

> —JEFF
> NEW YORK, NEW YORK

BE CREATIVE! For my girlfriend's birthday, I filled her cubicle at work with balloons, hung a dozen red roses from the ceiling, and arranged for a limousine to pick her up and take her to a spa for a day of pampering. It was so much better than simply buying a card and going out to dinner because it showed I was thinking about her and putting effort into the relationship.

—*ANONYMOUS*
CASTLE ROCK, COLORADO

HOLD OFF ON THE GIFT GIVING if it doesn't feel right to you. When I was living in L.A. I was dating this guy for about two months. He kept mentioning his upcoming birthday the week before and I felt that he was expecting something from me. Typically, I get in trouble for not doing enough in the relationship, so it's a bit ironic: I took him out to a really nice restaurant, may have spent $200 for the dinner. I think I even bought him something, too. It's really not like me to do these things so I got a bit mad when he wasn't very appreciative—it was as if he expected it. The next night was the birthday party that he was throwing for himself and I remember that he barely talked to me at all. It was horrible.

—*LAURA RICH*
BROOKLYN, NEW YORK

GIVE YOUR GIRLFRIEND'S PARENTS a thoughtful gift to get on their good side. My boyfriend worked for our college football team in Arizona and called the management office at the University of Nebraska—my parents' college team. He got a Nebraska game football and sent it to them. As they were huge Nebraska fans, that gift really buttered them up.

—*E.L.*
RENO, NEVADA

FIRST IMPRESSIONS ARE EVERYTHING

For our first date, I met the girl and her friends at a bar. When the waitress came to take our order, my date turned to me and demanded, "Aren't you going to buy me a drink?" This pissed me off, and I told her so. Her response? "When a guy is courting a girl, he needs to be the one buying the drinks." I'm an old-fashioned guy in general, and I agree with this statement. But I thought it was rude of her to demand it. So we got into a fight, during which she said, "Aren't you going to start a tab? I want to put my other drink on it, too." That's when I told her I was leaving to go talk to my friends, and I never came back.

This is 2004. If women want equal rights, they should at least offer to pay sometimes. Any decent guy will pay, but to not even offer— and, even worse, to demand that the guy pay—is a huge turn-off.

—*Dustin French*
Denver, Colorado

WHEN YOU GET A NUMBER, ASK HER when the best time to call her is. I don't take chances on that. I work too many hours and have too little free time to start adding on extra rules. I leave one message, and then I leave it up to her to call back.

—*CHAD MAKAIO ZICHTERMAN*
SAN FRANCISCO, CALIFORNIA

* * * * * * * *

DON'T EVER GIVE A GUY YOUR PHONE number right after you first meet him. Get his number, or set up a time to meet him somewhere. It is just safer, and then you don't end up with a stalker who calls you all the time. Then, don't give him your address or get in the car with him until you really feel comfortable that you know him. Come home alone!

—*PEGGY*
SEATTLE, WASHINGTON

* * * * * * * *

SEE THE PERSON YOU'RE DATING in as many situations as possible. For example, spend time with your friends, his friends, your family, his family, your co-workers, and his co-workers. Introducing your boyfriend to lots of different people, and spending time with them gives you many opportunities to observe him with others—and gives you feedback from others about him as well.

—*JAN*
ALLENTOWN, PENNSYLVANIA

* * * * * * * *

WOMEN LIVE AND BREATHE CLOTHES, so if you are well dressed, their impressions and assumptions about you will always be positive. You will also seem well-off, hygienic, healthy, professional, clean, well-mannered and not a serial killer.

—*P.W.*
HARRISONBURG, VIRGINIA

I firmly believe you should go Dutch, or else it sets up weirdness.

—*SCOOTER STRINGER*
SAN FRANCISCO, CALIFORNIA

DATING DATA

Garden snails court from 15 minutes to six hours. Part of the slow dance includes the snails shooting each other with special snail darts.

WOMEN IN THEIR 20S TEND TO BE PRETTY insecure—they're always cross-examining you about why you want to spend so much time with your buddies, and assuming your intentions are bad if you're not hanging out with them every second. By the time they reach their 30s, however, most women start feeling their biological clocks ticking and are more apt to accelerate the relationship: They don't get upset about so many little things and they give you a longer leash with your buddies.

> —*BILL CORRIGAN*
> *BOSTON, MASSACHUSETTS*

• • • • • • • •

DON'T DATE SOMEONE YOUR FRIENDS don't like. If they wouldn't want to be friends with the person, they probably see something you could be missing. My roommate has been dating someone we all refer to as "ass face," but she still can't see that there is something wrong with him. He's a complete meathead; it's starting to affect her friendships with some people. It sucks.

> —*MELISSA*
> *MANHATTAN BEACH, CALIFORNIA*

SEX: Not a Four-Letter Word

Should you or shouldn't you? On your first date—or your wedding night? Condom or pill? Does size really matter? And what's the best way to remove yourself from a bad-sex situation? The community weighs in.

IF I MEET SOMEONE AND WE HIT IT OFF beautifully, why should two consenting adults who want to become more intimate stop themselves? I don't feel that any arbitrary period of waiting is necessary if things are going very well between two people.

> —*STEVEN GLASSMAN*
> *DELRAY BEACH, FLORIDA*

GUYS SHOULD NEVER GIVE THEM-SELVES AWAY BY ASKING FOR SEX ON THE FIRST DATE.

—*MICHAEL AGEE*
SIMI VALLEY, CALIFORNIA

Finding someone physically attractive is not the same as being attracted to someone.

—*ANONYMOUS*
ANN ARBOR,
MICHIGAN

GOOD SEX IS JUST CHEMISTRY. It happens or it doesn't. You can't work at it. I've never gone out with someone and had a bad kiss and thought, "Oh, well, maybe the next one will be better."

—*C.V.*
NEW YORK, NEW YORK

• • • • • • • •

DON'T TAKE GIRLS HOME on the first night you meet them. I was with this girl once and we were fooling around and I wanted to have sex. She said, "Why me?" and I decided it was too much for me and I decided not to have sex. Then, she was asking me, "Why don't you want to do it with me." Don't try and have a one-night-stand unless you know both people are cool with it.

—*MICHAEL STENERSON*
DULUTH, MINNESOTA

I LOOK FOR "LINGERING." If she leans in to say something and stays close, that can be a sign. Of course, that could also be because we're in a noisy place, or maybe she likes the smell of my fabric softener, or the professor of the class she skipped this morning just walked into the cafeteria and she's moving behind me to remain hidden. Basically, anything short of a come-hither look or stripping leaves me with at least a few doubts.

—*CHAD MAKAIO ZICHTERMAN*
SAN FRANCISCO, CALIFORNIA

• • • • • • • •

SEX IS SOMETHING YOU CAN'T RUSH. It happens when both of you are ready. As Christians, my girlfriend and I know we're not ready. It's immoral. When you're married, that's the perfect time.

—*DOMINIQUE COLEMAN*
SYRACUSE, NEW YORK

STRANGEST PLACES TO HAVE SEX ...

THE MOST UNUSUAL PLACE I'VE HAD SEX is the bathroom at Café Greco. It was one of those look-at-each-other deals. I went to the bathroom and he came in a few minutes later. That was exciting.

—*D.*
SAN FRANCISCO, CALIFORNIA

OUR FRATERNITY RENTED A BUS for the Stanford-Cal game, and it was packed with people. I had sex with my girlfriend inside the bus bathroom, which was very difficult because it was so tiny and people kept banging on the door. My advice to anyone who wants to try this: go fast!

—*TIM G.*
BOULDER, COLORADO

I AM A BIG BELIEVER IN THE RULES—at least, for the first couple of weeks. However, I went out with this guy from work (Rule Breaker # 1) and on our first date we had such a great conversation that I invited him back to my apartment (Rule Breaker # 2) and ended up on my couch attacking him with kisses (Rule Breaker # 3). Not only did he end up staying the night (Rule Breaker # 4), but we ended up spending every day of the following week together (Rule Breaker # 5). That man is now my husband.

—*LISA*
MINNEAPOLIS, MINNESOTA

BE REALISTIC ABOUT OTHER PEOPLE'S expectations. There's nothing wrong with sleeping with someone that you just met if that's what you want and that's all you want. But be aware that it's not like any kind of guarantee of anything else. That's all it is.

—*LEILA*
WASHINGTON, D.C.

* * * * * * * *

❝Intimacy and kissing are personal. You should wait until you trust the other person and you just "can't wait" to take that step.❞

—*SHANA O'NEIL*
LAS VEGAS, NEVADA

* * * * * * *

AT FIRST, MAKE SURE YOU LEAD with your head and not your heart. Once you become physical, all objectivity goes out the window. It's better to make sure you have the same vision and goals before you get emotionally involved.

—*A.N.P.*
PITTSBURGH, PENNSYLVANIA

* * * * * * * *

Jump him. Just do it, 'cuz it's fun.

—*SYLVIA HOWELL*
BERKELEY,
CALIFORNIA

NOT ALL COURTSHIP LEADS TO MARRIAGE, which is the very reason one should never have sex while dating. Hold off on your passions: they are fleeting feelings. Don't blemish your wedding day by tasting the wedding cake before it's time to do so.

—*M.R.*
SYRACUSE, NEW YORK

KISSES CAN TELL

KISSES ARE A YUMMY PART OF GETTING TO KNOW SOMEONE, but it depends on the situation and the level of attraction and interest. The way someone kisses can tell you a lot about that person. The tentative peck on the cheek or lips, the smothering and all-consuming, the tender, or the fierce and invasive all give an indication of how thoughtful, caring (and experienced) the person is, and even, in some cases, the reason they are dating you. If they're all over you with their mouth and tongue in five minutes flat, they may be immensely attracted to you, or maybe just desperate for physical connection.

—*JENNY WHITE*
MALDON, VICTORIA, AUSTRALIA

• • • • • • • •

I DON'T KISS 'EM AT ALL UNLESS THERE'S CHEMISTRY. Kisses are too important to me. If there's chemistry, then I usually do it on the first date. Intimacy involves more discussion and paperwork (particularly, notes from doctors proving that he's disease free).

—*SARAH CLARK*
NEW YORK, NEW YORK

• • • • • • • •

A SIMPLE LITTLE KISS CAN BE ECSTATIC when the relationship is awash in ambiguity, and you just want some slight confirmation that things are headed in a physical direction. I've had a number of episodes with a transcendent first kiss, the most recent one being when I was living in New York, and the gentleman in question and I wandered around the Lower East Side, rambling about ourselves the whole time. He hailed me a cab and we met in an almost accidental, light as a feather, kiss on the lips. We both grinned like maniacs as the cab pulled away, with me inside, and him on the curb.

—*SHAUNA MCKENNA*
ST. PAUL, MINNESOTA

Big revelation: Alcohol is inextricably linked to sex.

—*BETTE CRAWFORD*
PHILADELPHIA,
PENNSYLVANIA

SOME OF MY FRIENDS WHO AREN'T on the pill just use condoms when they have sex. But I like using both. Don't depend on the other person in the relationship for birth control: I've been with guys who say they won't use condoms. One said, "I'm allergic to them." Your only response to that is: "Well, then I'm allergic to sex with you."

—*MINDY*
RICHARDSON, TEXAS

• • • • • • • •

SEX, ONE STEP AT A TIME

I was with one woman who followed "The Rules"—who let me kiss her on the first date, but not touch her breasts. On the second date, I could touch her breasts, but not her coochie. On the third, I could touch her coochie, but not have sex. And so I figured next time, I could have sex with her. But it turned out I had to sit through manual and then oral sex before I heard the preferred reply to the condom question.

—*LEE*
BROOKLYN, NEW YORK

• • • • • • • •

I've found that there is a pretty straightforward sex protocol that is observed in dating in New York, especially among girls I've met on Nerve.com and Jdate.com. Date Number One (if it goes well) is usually the make-out-in-the-bar-or-at-the-subway-platform-before-going-home date. Date Number Two is the I-the-girl-will-come-over-to-your-place-and-make-out-but-I-will-not-get-naked date. Date Number Three is the I-the-girl-will-come-over-get-naked-and-give-you-head-but-not-have-sex-with-you date. Date Number Four is a repeat of Date Number Three, and Date Number Five is usually the date when you have sex.

—*A.F.*
NEW YORK, NEW YORK

IF A WOMAN ISN'T READY TO HAVE SEX right away with someone, that's fine, but make sure you at least get into the kissing. It's an important cue to me, and maybe to other guys, that this is a sensual person who does like me, and that's a total turn-on.

—*BILL BRAZELL*
BROOKLYN, NEW YORK

• • • • • • • •

FOR THE GIRL, A GOOD PART OF THE DATING process is holding on to your morals and not giving in to the advances of the hot-blooded boy. And the easiest way to handle that is to let him know where you stand the first time he tries to put his moves on you. While I was dating this guy a couple years ago, I had to play some serious defense on just our second date. Then I told him that no matter how slick he was or how hard he tried it wasn't going to happen; I was not that kind of girl. He was disappointed, but I think he understood.

—*BARB G.*
PITTSBURGH, PENNSYLVANIA

• • • • • • • •

SEX IS A HUGE PART OF A RELATIONSHIP. In this day and age, I don't think you should go that long before sex if it means enough to you. I'd say three to four months is about the longest I would go, unless it was something really important to her.

—*STEVE SANDERS*
ATHENS, GEORGIA

• • • • • • • •

IF A GIRL WANTS TO HAVE SEX, she will make it obvious. She will always end up doing something stupid to let you know. She'll get drunk; start holding you; ask you stupid questions.

—*PANOS KOUTSOYANNIS*
SAN FRANCISCO, CALIFORNIA

Don't have sex. Recall those statistics about AIDS that we all learned back in elementary school.

—*LIZ HERTNECK*
WASHINGTON, D.C.

DATING DATA

According to an online survey of singles in their 40s, 50s and 60s, two percent of women say that sex is acceptable during the first date, and 20 percent of men think it is.

When in doubt, be aloof. Aloofness has the weird-but-useful property of drawing people to you and then, after coitus, pushing them away.

—*M.P.*
MIAMI, FLORIDA

THE DECISION TO NOT USE PROTECTION should always be an open discussion, usually backed up with HIV tests. This is not to be taken lightly. Never discourage any open dialogue. If your partner brings something up, hear him out.

—*ANONYMOUS*
NEW YORK, NEW YORK

· · · · · · · ·

I ALWAYS HAVE CONDOMS AT HOME, and I keep some in my car. My generation has grown up with them. I don't know anyone who doesn't have them in their nightstand. Nobody likes them. But if you understand the issue, you shouldn't care whether he likes them or not.

—*MEGAN RAMSEY*
PLANO, TEXAS

· · · · · · · ·

IT'S THE GUY'S RESPONSIBILITY to have condoms and the girl's responsibility to be on the pill if she doesn't want to get pregnant. When I was dating my old girlfriend and we didn't have a condom, I'd run out to get one because I knew it was up to me. There was one time I stumbled out of her bed at 2 a.m. so I would be prepared in the morning.

—*C.S.*
IOWA CITY, IOWA

· · · · · · · ·

DON'T MAKE A MOVE ON YOUR GIRLFRIEND while you are driving. I once leaned over to kiss my girlfriend at a stoplight, and my foot slipped off the brake and I hit the car in front of me. Not only did it not impress the girl, but the people I hit weren't too happy either. It was a pretty bad night.

—*BILL W.*
SEATTLE, WASHINGTON

DON'T ASSUME YOU CAN'T GET PREGNANT the first time you sleep with a new person. I met this guy at a bar on karaoke night. We instantly became friends, but he was much too needy, immature and financially unstable to date. After a couple months, I ended up having sex with him anyway when I was drunk, and we didn't use protection. This didn't bother me at the time because I assumed that since we didn't have a future together, nothing bad could possibly happen, right? WRONG! Always, always, always use a condom!

> —*RACHEL*
> *SEDALIA, COLORADO*

• • • • • • • •

THE BIGGEST MISTAKE I MAKE is letting my libido take the wheel. It's amazing how when you're so intensely physically attracted to someone, you rationalize all their glaring faults away—"Yeah, he has a drinking problem, but it's so cute on him!" or "The fact that he's been unemployed for over a year has just forced him to be a better cook!"

> —*HALEY*
> *ATLANTA, GEORGIA*

• • • • • • • •

SOMETIMES, IT'S ALL ABOUT COMPROMISE. This girl I was dating really wanted to have sex on a motorcycle—while it was moving. I said, "No way in hell," because it wasn't worth getting road rash down there if I wiped out. So instead we stopped the bike about 40 feet off the road and had sex in the middle of the desert on the bike while it was parked.

> —*J.C.*
> *REDMOND, WASHINGTON*

Knowing the right time to have sex for the first time is relative, but the first night usually isn't justified.

—*MIKEY*
CEDAR RAPIDS, IOWA

If you've found an easy way to bring up the subject of contraception, you're probably in that situation too often.

—BONNIE HOLMES, NEW YORK

GUYS SHOULD BE ATTENTIVE IN SEX. For me, when a guy just makes the effort to make me feel good, it does make me feel good. A lot of guys don't make the effort. They're purely in it for themselves. And if a guy makes me feel like he's more in it for me, then I'm more in it for him.

—AMY
ATLANTA, GEORGIA

• • • • • • • •

DON'T REVEAL SPECIFICS. Once, right after sex, I piped up and told a guy that he was lucky number 13 for me. Apparently, he didn't appreciate being told how many guys I had slept with or that he was number 13. I suppose it was a little tacky.

—LISA
MINNEAPOLIS, MINNESOTA

SEX-22

I think you should have sex whenever you want and not worry about the consequences. Unfortunately, in my life that has only resulted in "No second dates" since the men felt that they weren't special; that I sleep with everybody. That may have been true, but the double standard prevails and women, unless they meet that rare man with an ego to withstand it, are stuck with a "screw on the first date, no second date" outcome. I absolutely despise women who have given us a bad rap by refusing to put out until the third or fourth date, after a few free dinners and nights out. That's the ultimate in high–maintenance. It's not fair to men, who spend most of their lives paying for women without getting anything in return, and who endure most of the early relationship rejection. Men are a pain, but they suffer a lot to get laid—more than women ever will—and we should acknowledge this.

—ANONYMOUS
ATLANTA, GEORGIA

WHEN HAVING BAD SEX, FAKE IT. Mostly I just faked an orgasm or two as quickly as possible to get it over with. When it was bad, it usually involved inexperience, bad smells, or people who just didn't take direction very well.

—*SARAH CLARK*
NEW YORK, NEW YORK

· · · · · · · ·

JUST BECAUSE HE'S THE PERFECT GUY for you doesn't mean he doesn't have a rubber doll somewhere in his closet. This guy I used to date had one, and I had been seeing him for a while before he pulled her out of the closet so I could meet her. You think you know someone!

—*CINDY PFEFFER*
FOREST HILL, MARYLAND

· · · · · · · ·

HAVE RESPECT FOR THE PERSON you're dating or do not continue. I believe sex should come after marriage. If you love her, honor her. That's what I did. It is beautiful and you will be glad you did. Modesty is an important trait. It is something to preserve before and after marriage.

—*ANONYMOUS*
CIDRA, PUERTO RICO

· · · · · · · ·

PORN: MEN WATCH IT. It doesn't mean they don't think you're good enough or sexy enough. It's just a physical thing for them. Also, men masturbate even if they're sexually active. Don't take this as an insult and don't think you have the right to say he should stop. It's a way for men to have a "selfish" orgasm without having to worry or tend to others' needs. They still love you dearly and find you very attractive, I assure you.

—*CANDICE JACOBS*
WELCH, MINNESOTA

Sometimes women just want to get laid. Men don't understand that a woman might be attracted to them and not want a relationship.

—*ANONYMOUS*
CINCINNATI, OHIO

DATING DATA

At least 36 million people around the world are now infected with HIV ... and 75 percent of all new infections are transmitted through heterosexual contact.

If we've been together a while and I think we may have sex, I bring my own condoms. If I do that, I never wake up with that "Oh God, what did I do?" feeling.

—*Shana O.*
Las Vegas,
Nevada

Who hasn't had bad sex? Mostly it's been good because I consider myself a good communicator. I slept with someone once who couldn't seem to find the right parts. Funny, since she had the same ones.

—*J.A.*
Durham, North Carolina

· · · · · · · ·

Terrible sex came in many forms, from feeling like I'd just been kissed with a dripping wash-cloth, to lack of hygiene, to lack of ability, or being penetrated with such violence or lack of interest that it was just awful. Faking an orgasm is the best way out of the latter two situations.

—*J. M. Cornwell*
Tabernash, Colorado

· · · · · · · ·

Size does matter, but not as much as being a good lover. I once had sex with a man who had a two-inch penis when hard. That wasn't the bad part, though. With a straight face and with utter honesty, we could have worked around that particular bug had it not been for the fact that he was con-vinced he was the hottest thing around.

—*Christina*
Belmont, Massachusetts

· · · · · · · ·

After a five-minute fling, my guy held up a used condom and said, "It's full"—as if to com-pensate for his lack of endurance. That's the worst thing anyone has ever said to me after sex.

—*Lisa*
Des Moines, Iowa

BE PREPARED

YOU HAVE TO USE PROTECTION, but if you get caught without it, sometimes that can be for the best. Being condom-less, if you refrain from sex, can slow things and give you time to build the relationship before the next opportunity.

> —JESSE WOODRUFF
> WAYNESBORO, VIRGINIA

* * * * * * * * *

IF YOU ARE YOUNG, CHECK OUT PLANNED PARENTHOOD. First of all, it's a cheap place to get contraceptives; second of all, they won't tell your parents if you don't want them to tell. In my first lengthy relationship, sometimes we used condoms and sometimes we didn't. But I was on the pill, and we both got tested when we started dating, because he had cheated on his last girl-friend. I said, "Considering that you aren't that trustworthy, I want you to get tested." He went to his family doctor and he said his test came back clear. (I'd never thought about it, but maybe he never went. I didn't go with him; I just trusted that he did.)

> —ANONYMOUS
> WOOSTER, OHIO

* * * * * * * * *

IF YOU CARRY PROTECTION WITH YOU ON DATES, never keep it in the same place twice. I might put it in my jeans' pocket one time, in my wallet the second, and in my jacket the third. That way, if a girl ever stumbles upon it and accuses you of having bad intentions, you can prove her wrong next time, without being caught off guard.

> —ABIY WONDESSEN
> ETHIOPIA

Just say "no" to STD's and babies you aren't ready for!

—*L.B.B.*
Montreal,
Quebec, Canada

IF YOU HAVE A TINY PENIS, do not ask a girl to go down on you. You know it's tiny if it's the size of a Jolly Rancher. You don't have to be huge, by any means, to be good. I've dated lots of guys that had normal-sized ones and it's been great. But if a girl asks you, "Are you in yet?" then you have a problem. Of course, I also dated a guy who was too big. Every time we did it, I felt it in my throat.

　　　　—*Robyn*
　　　　　Atlanta, Georgia

• • • • • • • •

TOYS ARE FUN. I don't think guys are willing enough to bring in a vibrator: they should be, though. But don't surprise someone with it. I once had a guy whip out a vibrator. He wanted to surprise me with this little thing, but he didn't tell me about it. He just whipped it out and started using it. I was like, "Whoa." You have to talk about it first.

　　　　—*Amy*
　　　　　Atlanta, Georgia

Are you Serious? Getting Intense

Y*ou go on a date. Sparks fly. You go on a second date. You manage not to screw it up. A third date: wait, are you dating? What's that feeling in your chest? Why are you finding cheesy love songs to be particularly meaningful? Why are you thinking of something your date said and laughing to yourself because she's just so cute? Is she feeling the same way? It's the next step. Better keep reading.*

I AM A ROMANTIC. You pick up vibes or energy or something. I really believe you just know sometimes. Love is taking you and you are going on a ride whether you like it or not.

—PHIL S.
SAN FRANCISCO, CALIFORNIA

FOCUS ON HIS FAMILY. WHAT ARE THEY LIKE? THAT TOLD ME A LOT.

—LUBA FURTAC
CLIFTON, NEW JERSEY

Don't take your one-night stand home to your mom's house.

—*ANONYMOUS*
  WALNUT CREEK,
  CALIFORNIA

BECOMING BOYFRIEND AND GIRLFRIEND can sometimes be a little vague—there's no starting gun that goes off, announcing your boyfriend-girlfriend commencement. It's either very apparent—the two of you spend all of your time together and you really dig each other, so it's obvious that you'll date exclusively—or it happens in a conversation (Communication! Imagine that!) that you both agree that you want to only date each other.

> —*E.R.C.*
>   *CITRUS HILL, CALIFORNIA*

. . . .

DO THE INTRODUCTIONS WITH THE FAMILY sooner rather than later. I'm close with my parents, and my boyfriend and I lived near them, so my boyfriend met them after three weeks. My family is crazy. I think my boyfriend was quickly overwhelmed. But I figured that it was best that he knew about them. And it worked out well; they all get along.

> —*J.*
>   *CHESAPEAKE BEACH, MARYLAND*

. . . .

I'VE ALWAYS BEEN VERY RELUCTANT to let my girlfriends meet my family too soon. It's always an annual event with my cousins: Whom will they bring to Christmas this year? I never wanted to be like that and have my parents refer to my girlfriends as "the flavor of the month," so I waited a year to let my current girlfriend meet my parents and it worked out well.

> —*CHRIS*
>   *IOWA CITY, IOWA*

YOU HAVE TO BE COMFORTABLE with each other before meeting the parents of your girlfriend or boyfriend. I didn't meet my girlfriend's parents until six months into our relationship and it went very smoothly. They mostly just made fun of me for my southern accent, but overall it was fine—which it wouldn't have been if the meeting had taken place any sooner.

—EDDIE LEE
STATESBORO, GEORGIA

* * * * * * * *

ONE OF THE BEST TIMES TO INTRODUCE your girlfriend to the family is at big family events. I brought my girlfriend to my mom's retirement party after we were dating for six months. Before that, she had never met anyone in my family. It was a huge success. People are more open to meeting others at those kinds of events.

—ANDREW
EVANSTON, ILLINOIS

* * * * * * * *

PEOPLE SHOULD BE FRIENDS for at least two years before getting serious. We met on the Internet, so a long courtship gave us more time to know each other—and frankly, it was safer that way.

—AIDA S.
NEW ORLEANS, LOUISIANA

* * * * * * * *

RELIGION IS IMPORTANT TO ME, and it's something that has caused problems in the past. In high school, it wasn't as important to me to date someone who was of the same religion. When I got to college and started getting more into what I believed and started thinking about marriage, it became very important to me. It would make holidays interesting.

—A.W.
SWAINSBORO, GEORGIA

You know you are considered a member of the family when his grandmother gives you an Easter card with a $10 check inside.

—L.D.
OXFORD, OHIO

DATE PEOPLE THAT YOUR PARENTS LIKE—assuming, I guess, that you share your parents' values. Every guy I dated that my parents didn't like turned out to be a real creep in some way: One boyfriend cheated on me, another lied, etc. And the guys I dated that my parents approved of really did turn out to be nice guys, including my husband. Parents have marriages, relationships, and some life experience to draw from when they judge the people you date. So, bring those dates home to meet Mom and Dad!

—JULIE
SAN FRANCISCO, CALIFORNIA

☆

If you have a chance to meet the mother, do it. The way a guy treats his mother is the way he's going to treat you.

—STEPHANIE HACKER
SOUTH BEACH, FLORIDA

• • • • • • • •

ON THE FIRST DATE, I CAN TELL if there's chemistry. On Date Number Two, I can tell if we have enough in common to sustain a relationship. If we make it to Date Number Three, we're probably going to be exclusive. Obviously each situation is different, but I think people should trust their instincts on this one.

—SARAH CLARK
NEW YORK, NEW YORK

• • • • • • • •

MY ADVICE IS, DON'T GET INTO A RELATIONSHIP. You are selling your soul when you do this. Remain free, have fun, and stay out of commitments. They will ruin your life. I am as happy as can be dating a girl for a while and then moving on. It never gets boring and I can always bail. I do not worry about being alone. I have friends to hang with. I look for girls who do not want to commit, like me. I go to bars, use eye contact to send that "no commitment vibe" and the rest is artwork.

—ANONYMOUS
BLOOMFIELD, NEW JERSEY

FRIENDS AND LOVERS

BE SOCIAL WITH MUTUAL FRIENDS. Not only is it fun, but watching your partner interact with others can remind you why you fell in love.

—*SEEMA MATHUR*
ATLANTA, GEORGIA

• • • • • • • •

AS THE OLD SAYING GOES, "LOVE IS BLIND." It's also often deaf and dumb. But just because you're blinded by your love and often tune out all the bad things in your relationship, it doesn't mean your friends will. This is why it's best not to bad-mouth your boyfriend to all of your friends when you have the littlest fight, or spill his darkest secrets just for the sake of gossiping. You'll likely forgive and forget—but your friends won't. The last thing you want is to be at the altar when your friends decide they're not going to hold their peace—all because you told them about one mean thing he said or did.

—*LINDSEY GAWRON CALDWELL*
ARLINGTON, VIRGINIA

• • • • • • • •

I WAS DATING TWO GUYS at the same time. Then both relationships started getting more serious and time-consuming, and I really had to make a choice. But I still didn't know them all that well, and I liked them both. One of the deciding factors ended up being their friends. One of the guys just had the weirdest friends: I really didn't like any of them. The other one had fantastic friends, and I chose to keep seeing him. I eventually decided that the one with the friends I found weird was, himself, pretty weird. And the one with the fantastic friends was so fantastic, I ended up marrying him. And his friends that I love are now a regular part of my life, too!

—*SHANNON L.*
SAN RAFAEL, CALIFORNIA

KIDDIE CORNER

INTRODUCE YOUR CHILDREN AND YOUR DATE TO EACH OTHER. Children tend to have fantastic instincts. Trust them! You'll know if your date has no tolerance for children or if perhaps he's more interested in your kids than in you. Kids who are included have confidence and trust in you and your relationship with them. If they feel important, included, and respected, they might be less likely to try sabotaging a potential relationship.

> —*ANONYMOUS*
> *BEVERLY HILLS, CALIFORNIA*

MAKE SURE THE MAN YOU DATE wants to be around your children. That was what attracted me to my second husband. He tried to include the children when we dated. We would do things by ourselves, but then he'd say, "Let's take the kids out to dinner tonight." He'd say, "I have tickets to the circus; would the kids like to go?" We'd go on picnics, or go fishing, so that the children could get to know him. That was important.

> —*J.D.*
> *VANCOUVER, WASHINGTON*

AFTER BEING MARRIED TWICE, I think it is best not to introduce your kids to someone new until you're serious about the person you're dating—not while you're casually dating.

> —*ANONYMOUS*
> *CHICAGO, ILLINOIS*

MY BOYFRIEND HAS TWO KIDS. While they're little terrors sometimes, it's nice to come back after a long day and see their smiling faces. It's hard because we don't get to do everything we want all the time, but if you love the person, it shouldn't be a big deal.

> —*E.M.*
> *IOWA CITY, IOWA*

BE HONEST AND UPFRONT—tell your date that you have a child. Some people try to hide it. I told a boyfriend one time, "You know, it's a package deal." I don't remember why it came out that way. He said something that made me defensive: I was not going to forget my daughter just because this knight in shining armor came riding up. He was taken aback that I said it the way I did, but now that we're married, it's a big joke.

—*D.R.*
SYRACUSE, NEW YORK

• • • • • • • • •

I LEARNED THE HARD WAY to keep my relationships with men secret from my son, especially since he's not little any more. I had dated someone who became a real part of our family. He didn't stay around a long time, but long enough to break our hearts. My son has to be my first priority.

—*DEONA HOUFF*
MOUNT SIDNEY, VIRGINIA

• • • • • • • • •

YOU HAVE TO BE WILLING to make sacrifices. I'm divorced, and my 15-year-old son spends every other weekend with me, which means I can't sleep over at my girlfriend's house during those times. This was frustrating at first, but it quickly became a way of life. I accept the fact that my son needs a parent around. I can't leave him home alone. Sometimes, I make an effort to combine my two worlds—like by asking my girlfriend to join us for dinner—but I have never invited her to sleep over. There are some lines that shouldn't be crossed. I determined what they are by asking myself, "What kind of example would that be setting for my son?"

—*DOUGLAS MUTKA*
LITTLETON, COLORADO

MY CURRENT GIRLFRIEND TOLD ME she didn't think we were right for each other, but I wouldn't take 'no' for an answer. In the span of one year, she lived in Iowa, Washington, D.C. and Colorado. I hopped on a plane every other weekend just to see her and spend time with her. The girl must have gotten used to me because now I can't get rid of her. Whoever says persistence doesn't pay off must not be completely in love.

—*Buzz Orr*
Iowa City, Iowa

• • • • • • • • •

A TIGHTLY KNIT BOND

Look for someone you can trust—somebody you can tell your secrets to and not worry about how she's going to react to it. Honestly, the night I was asking her to be my girlfriend, I could have asked her to be my wife. I just knew. I don't know how to explain it. It was like we meshed. It was like a Kevlar vest. It's only strong because the mesh is woven so tight, and it fits so well together. Things fall through fishing nets. If you and your girlfriend are woven tightly, there's nothing that can break your bond. Sure, the physical attraction needs to be there, but it's not the most important thing. If you're just marrying somebody who has knockout gorgeous legs, what happens when they get into a car accident and lose their legs? There goes your attraction. I always thought it was a good saying: you marry your best friend.

—*Kevin Burns*
Syracuse, New York

TAKE IT SLOW AND BE UP-FRONT about your intentions. I was coming back from a conference and needed a ride from the airport. I called a woman my daughter babysat for. She picked me up and asked if I wanted to get something to eat. In the car, she gave me a card. I'm like, "What's this?" Basically, it was a nice card explaining that she was developing feelings for me and wanted to explore the possibility of a deeper relationship. "The only thing I ask is that you're honest with me," she said. That was the best thing she could have said. I told her I had just gotten out of a bad relationship and I wasn't going back into another one. She understood and suggested we just see what happened. So, we went to eat. Now, we're getting married.

—*THOMAS M.W. "MIKE" DOWNS*
FAYETTEVILLE, NEW YORK

• • • • • • • •

GUARD YOUR HEART AND EMOTIONS. Wait for the guy to make the first move. You don't want to get emotionally attached all at once. You can kind of tell when you're moving too fast, especially if after a month or two you're thinking about marriage.

—*LIZ*
ATLANTA, GEORGIA

• • • • • • • •

TAKE IT SLOW. My experience with dating is that I tend to get it ass-backwards. I usually have no desire in dating and then I get the chemical reaction, or chemical attraction, to someone and it gets too serious too soon and I find out later that he isn't a good match for me.

—*SARAH*
RALEIGH, NORTH CAROLINA

Keep living your own life—even if you think you've met Mr. Right. *Especially* if you think you've met Mr. Right!

—*M.E.*
FAIRFIELD,
CONNECTICUT

DATES TO REMEMBER

THE BEST DATE I EVER HAD WAS IN COLLEGE. We went to a restaurant at the inn where I worked. Our food was half price. I was encouraged to be myself, so I ordered ribs. We had a good meal, ended the night holding each other, and woke up with no regrets.

> —*SUGAR JOHNSON*
> *BROOKLYN, NEW YORK*

• • • • • • • •

MY DATE HAD ARRANGED FOR A VALENTINE'S DAY THEATER MATINEE to "Phantom of the Opera," dinner in a very posh hotel dining room and an overnight stay. Everything met my fantasy of a perfectly romantic date. It included good company, relaxed timing, great theater seats, good music, good food, dancing, attentive service, and more. I felt like he really listened to what I wanted and tried to please me.

> —*MARILYN BARNICKE BELLEGHEM*
> *BURLINGTON, ONTARIO, CANADA*

• • • • • • • •

MY BEST DATE INCLUDED DINNER, A PLAY, A GAME OF SCRABBLE (which I won), kissing for the 12 chimes of the clock at midnight, and watching "Scent of a Woman," all in one night. I guess the trick to finding your true love is endurance.

> —*E.F.J.*
> *IOWA CITY, IOWA*

• • • • • • • •

THE BEST DATE I EVER HAD WAS BACKPACKING with my wife-to-be at Desolation Wilderness. We were there for four days. We hiked across country, peed in the woods, and took frigid baths in Lake Aloha. We only saw seven people on that trip, all of them when we were on our way out of the woods.

> —*ALLAN JAFFE*
> *PETALUMA, CALIFORNIA*

THE BEST DATE I EVER HAD INVOLVED picking up my then-girlfriend (now wife) at work in Seattle and driving 150 miles south to a huge used bookstore called Powell's in Portland, Oregon. We took turns popping CDs into the machine. The store closed an hour after we got there, but we still got to browse a while and have coffee and dessert. On the way back we watched ice form on the antenna.

—*DAVID HUBBELL*
KIRKLAND, WASHINGTON

· · · · · · · · ·

A GUY I'D ONLY SEEN ONCE before picked me up for dinner and drove me up to a park. It was really dark, and as he took me through the woods, I began to get nervous. Then we came to a stream, and close to the water a blanket with candles had been set up. Next to that was a cooler that included wine and a wonderful dinner that he had cooked himself, complete with chocolate-covered strawberries for dessert. We ate under the moonlight, and I felt so special that someone had gone to all that trouble. I'd take a dinner like that over an expensive restaurant any day.

—*K.*
PALM BEACH GARDENS, FLORIDA

· · · · · · · · ·

ONE OF THE BEST DATES I EVER WENT ON was a spontaneous "walking date"—we must have covered five San Francisco neighborhoods. We said we'd meet for brunch at noon in the Haight and had no plans after that. Brunch was fun, so we walked though Golden Gate Park, then through the Richmond to Pacific Heights for a late-afternoon cocktail, and then to the Marina for dinner and a walk out to the water. It was a great way to spend a beautiful Sunday afternoon and evening.

—*DEBBIE M.*
CONCORD, CALIFORNIA

WHILE WE WERE DATING, my boyfriend and I took communication classes. It helped us to learn more about each other and enjoy each other more. We are now married, and we still use the information we learned. I encourage everyone to take these classes at the dating stage because you really learn a lot of helpful and fun techniques.

—*PATRICIA T.*
OAKLAND, CALIFORNIA

• • • • • • • •

❝Don't ever settle. Just because someone's interested in you doesn't mean you need to be interested in him. You never know when something better is going to come along.❞

—*AMY*
MARIETTA, GEORGIA

• • • • • • • •

I DON'T REALLY REMEMBER THE FIRST TIME I said, "I love you" to my girlfriend, whom I've been dating for two years. I think you get so caught up in the moment, that when no other words can describe how you feel being with that person, at that particular moment, you say it, but you're not thinking about saying it. It just happens. That's when you know.

—*CHRIS FARRINGTON*
LIBERTYVILLE, ILLINOIS

YOU SHOULD SAY "I LOVE YOU" when it echoes in your head over and over every time you're around that person—but you should also feel fairly confident they'll say it back.

—*LISA*
DES MOINES, IOWA

• • • • • • • •

ON THE SECOND DATE, I always take the person to the Clermont Lounge in Atlanta. If a date doesn't find it one of the most interesting slices of Americana there is, I don't think I'd find him interesting long-term. It's this dive strip club that plays rock music. People like Charlie Sheen and Mick Jagger go there. There's a stripper named Blondie who can crush a beer can between her boobs, and if someone gets out of hand, she'll do that and then chuck the can at the guy. There's even this dirty place on the ceiling tiles above the bar where the dancers always put their hands on the ceiling when dancing on the bar. They were serving Pabst Blue Ribbon in a can before it was trendy. My boyfriend and all the Georgia Tech people took me for the first time years ago—there's a dance floor for the college and live-music crowd, a live rock-and-roll band when the disco isn't playing, and then, of course, the odd, older, "can't get a job anywhere else" dancers— trying to dance to all of it on the bar. It's a great place.

—*C.B.*
ATLANTA, GEORGIA

I invite dates over to my apartment to watch *Spinal Tap*. It's one of my date tests. If you can get into *Spinal Tap*, you're worthy.

—*NANCY B.*
WASHINGTON, D.C.

A WOMAN ONCE SAID SHE LOVED ME very early on, after sex, and then apologized, saying it just slipped out. I've definitely almost had it slip out, too, way too early on, when I didn't really "love" the person. But the thing is, you can love someone in a few thousand different ways, so it's cool to say something like that whenever. But if you say it too early, before it's an obvious mutual feeling, you might lose the upper hand in the relationship.

—*LEE*
BROOKLYN, NEW YORK

⭐

Don't trust them until you have the ring.

—*CHANNING SALAMERA DANVILLE, CALIFORNIA*

• • • • • • • •

EVEN IF YOU THINK YOU ARE IN LOVE with somebody, you should definitely wait to say, "I love you." Feelings and emotions can be misleading. When you feel you are in love, step back and take some time to evaluate the person. Does she or he really make you happy? Really consider it. "I love you" is widely overused and misused.

—*GEORGE PAPPAS*
IOWA CITY, IOWA

• • • • • • • •

GIVE AFFECTION IN MODERATION. My boyfriend rarely says, "I love you." He doesn't hold hands and he never kisses in public. But, when he does say, "I love you," my heart flutters. I've learned to live without holding hands. And as for the kisses, well, I've become quite the thief.

—*K.D.*
JOHNSBURG, ILLINOIS

WHEN YOU SAY IT, MAKE IT SPECIAL. Make an impression so that she'll always remember it. Expressing that you love someone is more than just words. It's the actions that go with it. The first time I said, "I love you," I remember it was a big deal to say those words. I didn't say it until a few months into our steady dating. I had a friend of mine dressed as a chauffeur pick her up, blindfold her and drive her to meet me. I was at a gazebo in a park. The sun was setting. There was a pond. I was dressed in a suit with guitar and roses in hand. I played her a song I had learned, Extreme's "More than Words." The climax was "I love you." It was great. It took me a month to learn the song.

> —DREW
> SYRACUSE, NEW YORK

• • • • • • • •

DON'T FREAK OUT ABOUT WHEN TO SAY, "I love you." There's no right timetable for these words. My husband told me he loved me two weeks into our relationship, when we were hiking Mt. Holy Cross in Colorado. You could tell it just sort of slipped out of his mouth instinctively, because right after he said it, he got this embarrassed, "Oops, I didn't mean to say that!" grin on his face. But I'm glad he did, because for us, the timing felt right.

> —WREN JOHNSON
> CENTENNIAL, COLORADO

• • • • • • • •

✔ **WHEN YOU'RE EXPRESSING YOUR LOVE** for someone, tell him why in a note or card. List the reasons you love them. You could also include the things that he sometimes does that you appreciate (like chewing with his mouth closed).

> —K.S.
> SPRINGFIELD, ILLINOIS

DATING DATA

W Network says when a woman is meeting her boyfriend's parents, a good present to bring is a book that she likes. It's a good conversation starter.

YOU KNOW YOU'RE SERIOUS

...when you can call the other person "babe" and they don't laugh.

> —SETH
> NEW ORLEANS, LOUISIANA

• • • • • • • •

...when the person you're dating takes you to meet his parents.

> —MEGAN
> CASTLE ROCK, COLORADO

• • • • • • • •

...when you look through the list of people you've called on your cell phone, and the last ten numbers are all the same.

> —EMILY
> LOUISVILLE, KENTUCKY

• • • • • • • •

...when you run out of minutes on your cell phone.

> —STUART MAZANEC
> LARKSPUR, COLORADO

• • • • • • • •

...when you're introduced to friends as someone's boyfriend or girlfriend.

> —LUCAS WINDER
> CASTLE ROCK, COLORADO

• • • • • • • •

...when you and he have special screen names so you can IM each other privately, in secret.

> —N.
> BROOKLYN, NEW YORK

DON'T OVERANALYZE A DATING SITUATION. When I was 23, I started dating a 34-year-old man whom I didn't tell anybody about, because I was afraid the age difference would make me look like a hussy. I secretly worried what my parents would think and questioned what his motives were. After all, I was just a dumb little girl, and he had all this life experience. I assumed he must be sleeping with several other women on the side. After all, why would he want to be serious with me? Needless to say, things didn't work out because I never gave our relationship a chance to develop. This is one of my bigger regrets—I wish I could've been more secure with myself and less suspicious of him, because I really think we had the beginning of something special. Once you get out of college, age is just a number anyway. Go with the flow, and enjoy it!

> —*NIKKI KING*
> *BEVERLY HILLS, CALIFORNIA*

• • • • • • • •

IF YOU WANT TO HAVE "OUR SONG," pick one that has meaning. Our song was "What a Wonderful World," by Louis Armstrong. My boyfriend asked me to be his girlfriend the day before his cousin was getting married. At the wedding, the first dance we had was to that song. After that, that was just our song when it came on. We made CDs for each other. He would put it on my CD, and I'd put it on his. It became a very significant song. That song makes me think about how awesome God is and how incredible it is to have someone to share your life with.

> —*TERI BURNS*
> *SYRACUSE, NEW YORK*

DATING DATA

According to AskMen.com, when you meet your girlfriend's parents, the top conversation topics to avoid are jokes, politics, personal questions, religion, money or income.

LEARN TO APPRECIATE LOVE for what it really is. Hollywood has given us a definition of love that for many people is unrealistic, and we are often so busy waiting for the pre-defined, and often inapplicable, signs of love that we ignore the

truly meaningful moments. I had a boyfriend of two years whom I got along with excellently and who made me very happy. However, he never did any of those spontaneous and wonderful things that "movie boyfriends" (and sometimes real-life ones) do. For a long time I thought that he didn't love me because he failed to buy me flowers and shower me with compliments. However, when I found myself in a hospital alone in a foreign country, he was the one by my side, taking care of the paperwork, sleeping on a plastic chair by my bed and calling my mother to calm her down. These are the meaningful things, the true signs of love that a million flowers cannot pretend to be.

—*REBECCA KAZZAZ*
BETHESDA, MARYLAND

• • • • • • • •

MUSIC ADDS TO THE MEMORY. When you look back, songs help remind you of that time. We had a song that we both liked. He proposed to me with that song playing. It was Norah Jones's "Come Away With Me." He made a digital video of us, with the song playing in the background. The song talks about coming away to a mountaintop. I just pictured the two of us climbing a mountain together, reaching the top, and kissing. Later, we actually got to climb a mountain together and live out that dream.

—*SARAH R.*
BOSTON, MASSACHUSETTS

I THINK IT'S GREAT IF COUPLES HAVE "their song." When my wife and I were first dating, I put together a CD of some songs that I thought she'd enjoy. I included a song, "When You Say Nothing at All," that always made me think of her. When I gave my wife the CD, she was shocked. It turns out that independently she had heard that song, too, and considered it "our song" as well.

—MICHAEL
HELLERTOWN, PENNSYLVANIA

MY HUSBAND AND I HAVE a special place in our hearts for Billy Joel's song, "Just the Way You Are." On our first date, we were in a bar that had a cheesy singer who did the sappiest rendition of that song. We just looked at each and laughed, and it made us both so comfortable, like we we'd known each other forever. I don't know if I can say that I knew from that moment he was The One but I can say that it made us feel instantly connected. When we want to cheer each other up, one of us will just start singing that in a lounge-singer way, and it cracks us up.

—S. COLEMAN
NEW YORK, NEW YORK

WHEN MY HUSBAND AND I WERE FIRST dating, we went to see *An American in Paris*. I had always wanted to have a song with Andy, and when we heard the song, "Our Love Is Here To Stay," it struck a chord in each of us and we decided it would be our song. Now when we hear it, we kind of smile at each other.

—D.B.
TENAFLY, NEW JERSEY

I don't think political views conflict with relationship views. My girl-friend isn't die-hard right, but her uncle is a well-known Republican fig-ure, so she generally sides with the right and I side with the left, but everything seems to go OK.

—RYAN SIEVEKING,
ATHENS, GEORGIA

EVERY COUPLE SHOULD HAVE A SPECIAL song as a way to reconnect with each other. Ours is "Mission of My Soul," by Peter Himmelman. We both like it and if you asked us each independently what song reminds one of us of the other, that's the song we'd say. Whenever we hear it, we stop what we're doing and just dance.

—*M. & M.*
KIRKLAND, WASHINGTON

• • • • • • • •

OUR SONG IS "SEVEN NATION ARMY" on the album *Elephant* by The White Stripes. We went to a restaurant, and we heard that song and realized we both liked it. It was our first date. The song started a great conversation about music, and we went from there. We got married about a year and a half later.

—*LENG-SUI WONG*
TAINAN CITY, TAIWAN

• • • • • • • •

MY EX-GIRLFRIEND AND I NEVER HAD "our song." She kept pestering me that we should have one, but the more she pushed, the more irritated I got. So I dumped her. I told my wife that story when we were dating, and she's never bugged me to come up with "our song." (Oh, I'm sure it was about more than just the song, but still, it just seems so artificial that everyone feels like they have to have "our song.")

—*PAUL*
MINNEAPOLIS, MINNESOTA

11

The Big Cs: Commitment and Cohabitation

*Y*ou *found someone you love so much you don't want to spend a moment apart. Where do you go from here? Is it time to move in together, or will that end the magic? Here are tips on how to handle your ever-evolving relationship.*

LIVING TOGETHER TAKES SOME of the romance out of combining your lives in a newlywed sort of way. But it's just so much more practical to know what you're getting yourself into. I already knew my boyfriend leaves wet towels on the bed, wiggles his legs and snorts in his sleep and leaves the dirty dishes in the sink until he can smell them from another room. That may have knocked some of the luster off his image, but it let me decide whether or not these are things I could learn to live with before the deal had been set in stone.

—*K.R.*
LOS ANGELES, CALIFORNIA

ALLOW EACH OTHER TIME AND SPACE ALONE. IT EASES THE TRANSITION.

—*SARA D.*
FREDERICK, MARYLAND

A relationship can work only if two people want the same thing.

—*KELLY*
  SAN FRANCISCO,
  CALIFORNIA

IT'S OK TO MOVE IN WITH SOMEONE when you know for sure you want to be with each other through the end of the leasing cycle. Theoretically. And if you're spending all your time together anyway, paying rent on two apartments is a pretty big luxury if it's just for the sake of maintaining the semiotics of independence.

—*BETTE CRAWFORD*
  PHILADELPHIA, PENNSYLVANIA

• • • • • • • •

IF I HADN'T BEEN USED TO LIVING WITH HIM, I would have left after we got married. But because we shared a place and our lives before we were married, I already knew that he's just like his dad sometimes and says stupid-ass stuff and then feels bad five minutes later. Now I can let it go.

—*ANONYMOUS*
  EL DORADO, KANSAS

• • • • • • • •

MY MESSAGE TO ANYONE OUT THERE: Please make sure you are married or about to be married before you move in with someone. I made that mistake and I am paying for it big time.

—*B.J.*
  BROOKLYN, NEW YORK

• • • • • • • •

LIVING TOGETHER ISN'T AS HARD as people think, unless you're a control freak (or your roommate is). Don't expect a slob to change just because you constantly nag about cleaning up. Don't expect a meticulous cleaner to relax just because you explain that a certain amount of bacteria is natural.

—*L.*

WE MOVED IN TOGETHER BECAUSE we wanted to be around each other all the time and I was sick of driving back and forth from his place. It's like 45 minutes without traffic. With traffic, it's like an hour and 15 minutes. It was a real pain. For me, a lot of it had to do with logistics. But one thing changed between us when we moved in together, and it was unexpected in a good way. I thought we were already really close. And I didn't expect there to be any changes to the way our relationship works. But living together has brought us closer together. Our relationship is more integrated now than it was before. We're more a part of each other's lives than we were before.

—*ANONYMOUS*
ATHERTON, CALIFORNIA

• • • • • • • •

DON'T LIVE WITH SOMEBODY out of necessity. I lived with one boyfriend who had lost his job at a newspaper and got a job in Louisiana, so we moved in together there. It was a drama after we broke up.

—*P.J.*
NEW YORK, NEW YORK

• • • • • • • •

I LIVED WITH MY BOYFRIEND MY SENIOR YEAR of college. My parents were thrilled because it meant half the amount of rent I was planning to pay myself. A lot of people say it's a good idea to live with someone before you end up getting married to see how you are together. In my case, it made me realize that there was no way I wouldn't want to live with my boyfriend in the future. You have to try it to believe it.

—*SARA*
CHICAGO, ILLINOIS

BETTER NOW THAN LATER

LIVING TOGETHER NOW CAN SAVE YOU FROM DIVORCE LATER. I lived with a girlfriend, and although things were going well, I started to realize over time that I loved her for many things but simply didn't have the romantic passion for her that I wanted to have. I realized this after we had lived together for a few months. When I broke up with her, it was sad and difficult. She was so angry with me and her parents were furious with me as well. I know it was hard, but it was better than getting married and then realizing the passion wasn't there later. In the end, living together was helpful because we got to know each other much faster than if we had kept dating and living separately. It would have been horrible if we had gotten engaged a year later without living together and then got divorced eventually.

—*KENT M. ZIMMERMANN*
CHICAGO, ILLINOIS

- - - - - - - -

LIVING TOGETHER BEFORE MARRIAGE is a good idea, because it gives you the chance to experience what married life is going to be like on a daily basis. It also gives you insight into certain things about the other person that you might not have picked up on otherwise. My girlfriend is obsessed with making sure everything is spic and span, whereas I'm kind of a slob. She is also capable of running a household—fixing leaky sinks, decorating rooms, planting gardens and flowers—which is good, because I like to be taken care of, just like any guy.

—*DOUG BRIMMER*
COLORADO SPRINGS, COLORADO

DON'T GIVE UP GOOD HOUSING and move in with a guy until you are really, really sure you'll be staying together. I had the best roommates, and such a great, cheap deal, and I gave it up to move in with a boyfriend. Half a year later, I didn't have the boyfriend, but I was saddest that I no longer had the great roommates and cheap deal!

—*J.B.*
SAN FRANCISCO, CALIFORNIA

• • • • • • • •

DATING DETAIL

Do you suffer from Gamophobia? If so, you are pathologically afraid of marriage.

IF YOU ARE THINKING ABOUT MOVING IN together, make sure you know what you are getting into. It's not a casual thing, and it really changed things in my relationship for the worse. We weren't close friends, only lovers. Now I know that to live with someone, it's much better if you are friends, too. Otherwise, there's only so much fooling around you can do before you get on each other's nerves.

—*ZINNIA*
HOBOKEN, NEW JERSEY

• • • • • • • •

OUR BIGGEST CONCERN AFTER MOVING IN TOGETHER was that when you're around someone all the time you take them for granted more. You shouldn't do that. Before we moved in together, I used to hang out at his house a lot. He would travel a lot, and if I hadn't seen him in a couple of days, I would be very excited to see him, sort of like a puppy dog greeting him at the door. He liked it. It gets harder to do that after you've moved in together, but I still try to do things that show him I don't take him for granted. I still make the effort to greet him at the door. The things he likes a lot, I try to do. I put my work down and pay attention to him.

—*ANONYMOUS*
ATHERTON, CALIFORNIA

MY GIRLFRIEND AND I LIVED TOGETHER for almost a year while we were engaged, and her parents still don't know about it. They are very old-world. Even now that we're married, with a kid, I think they'd disapprove of us having lived together then. It was a pain and it was expensive to hide it. I had to store my furniture, and we had to keep separate phone lines. It was exhausting living the lie.

—*JOHN KIM*
LOS ANGELES, CALIFORNIA

• • • • • • • •

THE ONLY MAJOR ADJUSTMENT WAS that I'm a big sports fan and she doesn't like sports. So I don't watch it as much anymore. Every Sunday was football day in the past, but now I have to pick. It used to be that I'd even watch the University of the Pacific vs. Hawaii at 2 a.m. Now I have to just watch my main teams, like the Colts, when they're nationally televised.

—*JON JONES*
ZIONSVILLE, INDIANA

• • • • • • • •

The number of carats in the diamond is the number of babies I'll have.

—*N.L.*
CHICAGO, ILLINOIS

YOU HAVE TO DEAL WITH WEIRD idiosyncrasies when you move in with someone. My boyfriend and I moved in together and the little things showed up—like, the fact that he's a Diet Coke fiend. He'll drink five or six a day and leave the cans all around the house. He sets them wherever he happens to be. I'll find them on top of the mantle or the bathroom sink. The only way to deal with that and keep a good relationship is through humor. I'll find a can and say, "Oh, look, the Coke fairy left us a present!" It annoys him, but he'll throw it in the recycling bin.

—*J.*
CHESAPEAKE BEACH, MARYLAND

COMPROMISE IS YOUR FRIEND. As much as compromise is your friend, working on both sides of the compromise is also your friend. Don't always be the compromiser. Get your way sometimes, although not always. For example, if your significant other would like to stay in, and you would like to go out, figure out which one is more desperate in their need, and go with that one. It goes both ways.

> —*XAVIER V.*
> *PITTSBURGH, PENNSYLVANIA*

· · · · · · · ·

"It is not the time to pop the question when you've had to stay up nights in perpetual turmoil trying to talk yourself into it."

> —*A.R.T.*
> *SAN FRANCISCO, CALIFORNIA*

· · · · · · · ·

I THINK IT'S GREAT TO LIVE WITH SOMEONE before you're married. It's a test of your relationship. If you can't live together, you shouldn't be getting married. That's what happened to me with my ex-fiancé. We lived together and he ended up breaking it off.

> —*PEGGY*
> *ST. PETERSBURG, FLORIDA*

EXPECT THE UNEXPECTED

It can't always be about you. You have to think about the other person on a regular basis to make things work. How will he respond to something I say or something I do? What does he need from me? One example was Valentine's Day this year. For months I had been looking forward to a whole day alone with my boyfriend. He lives two hours away, so we don't get to see each other often. It was supposed to be our time.

But instead of spending it the way we wanted to, we ended up spending the day dealing with a family crisis. We spent eight hours with them that Saturday, and yet I didn't really feel like it was my business being there because it was his side of the family. After a few hours of discomfort—everyone was sad and crying—I realized that it wasn't about me. I might have been uncomfortable, but what my boyfriend needed was for me just to be there to support him. It might not have been the most ideal or romantic way to spend Valentine's Day, but that doesn't matter. This is the way he needed me then, and I was happy to be there.

—E.J.
ST. LOUIS, MISSOURI

MY ADVICE IS, DEFINITELY LIVE TOGETHER before you get married. When you're seriously dating and thinking about marriage, the conversation is great, the sex is great, and just hanging out is great, but you can always escape to your own space. You might be deeply, madly in love, but that's no guarantee of compatibility. You don't want to find out the day after your honeymoon whether you can actually live together or not.

—*D.E.*
FT. WALTON BEACH, FLORIDA

. . . .

THE KEY TO LIVING WITH A SIGNIFICANT other is to work around each other's schedules. She's a teacher and up at 5:30 a.m., and half the time I don't go to work until after noon. This way, we don't get in each other's hair. If you are constantly with the other person, it won't work.

—*S.R.*
LAKEMOOR, ILLINOIS

. . . .

DON'T RUSH INTO LIVING TOGETHER. I will not live with someone again until I'm married. It's a boundary issue now. When I was younger, I wasn't worried about the future, and living together seemed safer—because it seemed like you're testing the waters and there's less commitment. But I'm now in a place in my life that in order for me to be that emotionally vulnerable, I need the extra commitment in return.

—*K.R.*
LOS ANGELES, CALIFORNIA

Get married—then continue dating your spouse.

—*PAUL*
BERKELEY HEIGHTS, NEW JERSEY

HANG ON TO YOUR FRIENDS

WHEN YOU START DATING SOMEONE, your first reaction (due to the butterflies that begin to accumulate in your stomach and perhaps filter to your head) is to spend all of your time with that person and basically drop your close friends. Don't do it! Maybe the relationship will work, maybe it won't. Either way, you will need those good friends to get you through it, whether you want to kill him and need help hiding the body or you need bridesmaids for your wedding!

   —*L.*
     COLUMBIA, MISSOURI

· · · · · · · · ·

IN ONE RELATIONSHIP THAT I HAD IN COLLEGE, I got so caught up in my boyfriend that I ignored all of my freshman year friends. Looking back now, I know that my boyfriend and I were far too serious. He was also very jealous, even with my female friends. By my junior year, my friends were tired of me dissing them. I regret that now, because I don't have those friends anymore. They wrote me off.

   —*J.*
     SHOEMAKERSVILLE, PENNSYLVANIA

· · · · · · · · ·

WHEN YOU'RE YOUNG, IT'S EASY to become consumed with the person you're dating. My daughter was once so head-over-heels with a boyfriend that she lost touch with many of her friends. It's better to have distance. If you get too consumed, you forget about your friends. Or if you have a weaker personality, you latch on far more than is healthy. It builds strength in your relationship to have friends. Plus, if the relationship ends, it's your friends who will help you pick up the pieces.

   —*W.F.*
     MERTZTOWN, PENNSYLVANIA

WHEN I STARTED DATING MY BOYFRIEND, I stopped spending time with my friends. So did he. We didn't plan to ignore our friends, but we only wanted to be with each other. Eventually, my friends stopped calling and inviting me out with them. My parents warned me that I would need and miss my friends even if I married Tom. I didn't listen to them, but they were right. I lost a lot of good friends because of my foolishness. And I sure missed them after I got married. I needed my girlfriends to talk to!

—*ANONYMOUS*
WILLIAMSBURG, VIRGINIA

- - - - - - - -

FRIENDS ARE FOREVER BUT MEN COME AND GO. I'm in a long-term relationship now, and the way we keep it going is to value our other friendships as much as we do each other. If you're not careful to keep your friends, you'll lose them. The fact that we hang out with our friends separately gives us both a sense of our own identity in the relationship.

—*LINDSEY L.*
IOWA CITY, IOWA

MY HUSBAND AND I DIDN'T LIVE TOGETHER before getting married because I'd read so many articles that claimed the divorce rate was higher for couples who did. After our wedding, we truly felt like newlyweds. Learning to live with each other's quirks (and discovering what those quirks were) adds fun to your first year of marriage.

—KARA JOHNSTON
KLAMATH FALLS, OREGON

Don't settle down before age 30. Love will always be there when you want it later, and women will always be ready to settle down.

—KENNY
NEW YORK,
NEW YORK

BE READY TO BE A GROWN-UP. I lived with a boyfriend twice. I was so young—23 and 24. I was engaged to one of them. We moved in together. I realized we were going to be grown-ups. It was not what I wanted so I broke it off. I don't think he was terribly happy about that. I saw him a year later and he was still pissed off.

—DEANNA ABNEY
SAN FRANCISCO, CALIFORNIA

THE MINIMUM AMOUNT OF TIME two people should date before marriage? Two years. I'll qualify that by saying two years if they live in the same city. Four years if the couple is dating long distance. My former husband and I dated for two years. However, at the time, we were living in different states—I was in Texas, and he lived in Louisiana. To stay in contact, we mostly wrote letters. We simply didn't have the money to telephone. We got married after we graduated from college. Looking back, I realize that we didn't know each other well enough simply because we didn't have enough contact during our courtship.

—MELLANESE LOFTON
WAIKOLOA, HAWAII

FIGHTING THE GOOD FIGHT

IT'S SO BORING to be in a relationship with someone that you can't argue with.

—*FRANCESCA*
ATLANTA, GEORGIA

• • • • • • • •

REMEMBER THAT YOU CAN'T TAKE BACK WORDS OR BEHAVIOR. People may forgive, but they never forget.

—*C.S.*
SAN FRANCISCO, CALIFORNIA

• • • • • • • •

DON'T SAY HURTFUL WORDS IN ANGER. They can never be erased and the wound will always remain. Always be respectful. Never, even in an argument, cross that line. In a past relationship, I told my boyfriend I was no longer attracted to him. Then we could never work things out because he never felt confident about himself after that.

—*K.*
ATLANTA, GEORGIA

• • • • • • • •

I STILL APPRECIATE A GOOD PILLOW FIGHT. I lived with a guy for two years—we were continually working on stuff, so the occasional pillow fight was a great way to let off steam!

—*AUDREY*
BENICIA, CALIFORNIA

• • • • • • • •

IF YOU'RE PISSED OFF, it's better just to be pissed off and yell at the person than to hold it all in.

—*ANONYMOUS*
BALTIMORE, MARYLAND

IF IT FEELS RIGHT, TAKE THE PLUNGE. I dated my husband for only six months before we got married. I realize that, by today's standards, we married quickly. But I just "knew" he was the right person when I met him.

—*JAYNE J.*
TULSA, OKLAHOMA

• • • • • • • •

YOU ONLY ASK HER TO MARRY YOU ONCE, so make it memorable. Have fun and be creative. About a week before I proposed, I secretly planted notes every day for my girlfriend to find, leaving her wondering and guessing. I had written, "Will you marry me?" on the back of a puzzle. With each note I left for her to find, I included a few puzzle pieces. With the last note, she got the final pieces that revealed my question. It worked. She said yes.

—*KEVIN SHOLANDER*
FORT COLLINS, COLORADO

• • • • • • • •

ENGAGEMENT SHOULDN'T COME as a total surprise. You should have had conversations about the future, but the actual moment you ask her to marry you should be this epic romantic moment that she doesn't necessarily see coming.

—*A.R.T.*
SAN FRANCISCO, CALIFORNIA

HEED THE SIGNS

Three clues your man is not ready for marriage:
1. He refers to his married friends as "losers."
2. He repeatedly makes you cry.
3. He buys a sports car.

THE BEST GIFT I GOT WAS an engagement ring. It was a Saturday. I thought he was working, but he had the day off. Some friends of ours were in on the plot. I was supposed to baby sit that day: they got me out of it. We ate dinner and were hanging out. The doorbell rang. I opened the door and I saw our other friend standing in the driveway with a video camera, then I saw my boyfriend's mom. Then my boyfriend came up to the door holding a huge pumpkin in his hands. It was all lit up, and it said, "Will you marry me." He put the pumpkin down and got down on one knee and told me I was special and he wanted me to be his wife. The ring that he gave me was his grand-mother's, so it has special meaning. It was very cool.

—*TERI BURNS*
SYRACUSE, NEW YORK

• • • • • • • •

I TOLD ONE GIRLFRIEND I WANTED TO SEE other women and she said it was all or nothing. So I chose nothing and broke up with her. Another girlfriend said it was OK and we both dated other people casually for a while. We ended up decid-ing we just wanted to date each other after all. We're married now!

—*J.W.*
ROCHESTER, NEW YORK

READ THE SIGNS

Three clues your man might be ready for marriage:

1. He feels he has sowed all his oats.
2. He wakes up one day and wants to be a dad.
3. He's financially secure.

BEST LOVE STORIES

Recharge your dating batteries with one of these good reads:

Romeo and Juliet by William Shakespeare

Jane Eyre by Charlotte Brontë

The Thorn Birds by Colleen McCullough

A Farewell to Arms by Ernest Hemingway

Persuasion by Jane Austen

Wuthering Heights by Emily Brontë

Anna Karenina by Leo Tolstoy

And if you don't need to impress anyone, try one of these:

Love Story by Erich Segal

Mistral's Daughter by Judith Krantz

Message in a Bottle by Nicholas Sparks

Like Water for Chocolate by Laura Esquivel

Rocky Roads: Trouble Ahead?

I *t can happen at any dating moment. You get that "uh-oh" feeling; a clench in your gut, a buzzing in your head like a car alarm. Whether it's a first date or a last dance, when that red flag goes up, you've got Trouble, my friend. Read some tales of woe below, and be sure none of these horror stories ever happens to you.*

WARNING SIGNS ON THE FIRST DATE: Your date endlessly talks about his or her problems; frequently mentions his or her ex; mentions, even once, the person he or she is currently involved with; seems bitter or mean-spirited; jokes about things that make you extremely uncomfortable.

—STEVE DAMON
MANCHESTER, PENNSYLVANIA

THE WORST THING THAT EVER HAPPENED TO ME ON A DATE WAS HAVING MY **ATM** CARD STOLEN— BY MY DATE!

—MIKE
DENTON, TEXAS

NOT YOUR PURR-FECT DATE

I found a man online who was handsome in his picture. He described himself as 5'11", muscular, good-looking. He said he was a doctor. We had similar interests, so I e-mailed him. We exchanged e-mails for about a week. He seemed like he had a good sense of humor. We agreed to meet for coffee. I was running about 15 minutes late, and I swear he called me six times on my cell phone. That should have been a tip-off right there. I got to the coffee shop and looked in the window. I could see a guy who sort of looked like the picture—but 5'8" on a good day, and feather-light! I mean, waifish, fragile! But I figured, what the heck, I've got nothing going on, so I went in. Right from the start, the conversation was stale—he's gave me one- or two-word replies. He asked me if I had a car. I said yes, did he? No. He never learned to drive. "Did you grow up in the city?" No, he grew up in Arizona. His parents sent 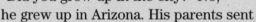 him to reform school in New York City, and sent his twin brother to reform school in Virginia. So I jokingly asked, "What did you do, skin a cat?" He replied, "Just one—meow." I chugged that coffee like athletes chug Gatorade in the commercials and got out of there.

—*Jennifer T.*
New York, New York

I WAS AT A DANCE AND THIS GUY comes up and wants to dance. He was sweating horribly, but I still said, "OK." We were dancing, and as he goes to twirl me, he grabs hold of my earring by accident and rips it out. I screamed in pain, and my earring went flying across the room. My advice: When you ask a girl to dance, make sure you know how.

> —*MAJA B. GERDIN*
> *SAN ANTONIO, TEXAS*

• • • • • • • •

I WAS DATING THIS GIRL and she came into a bar where I worked with a girl friend. At one point I looked over and she was making out with the other girl. And so I tapped her on the shoulder and said, "What's up?" And she was like, "Oops." I had no idea that she was bisexual. That's most guys' fantasy, but when it happens to you, it's sort of shocking. You think you know someone, but you don't.

> —*J.S.*
> *ATLANTA, GEORGIA*

• • • • • • • •

I MET MY FUTURE WIFE'S PARENTS at a pool party. The parents were there with all the neighbors. Well, before I made my grand entrance, I had ordered a Coke and the server had put an extra long straw in the glass. We went through the gate to the party and the gate squeaked loudly so everyone turned to see who was coming in. Right at that moment, I took a nervous drink of my Coke and the straw went straight up my nose and it started bleeding profusely. That's how I met her parents. They never liked me after that.

> —*MICHAEL AGEE*
> *SIMI VALLEY, CALIFORNIA*

Beware of boyfriends who are very close to their mothers. One of my old boyfriends had a mom who didn't like me and it ruined the whole thing.

—*S.M.*
HIGHLAND PARK, ILLINOIS

LADIES, BEWARE

Any man emerging from a serious relationship, no matter how stable he seems to be, definitely merits a giant caution flag. There was a guy I was interested in for a long time, but he was in a serious relationship with a girlfriend. One day he said he and his girlfriend had broken up and he asked me out. My friends cautioned me, but we went out on a date. We dated for a while. Things went well but I could tell he had reservations at times. Though he denied it, I felt he still had feelings for his ex. We had a long, serious conversation and he assured me everything with his ex-girlfriend was behind him. He convinced me. I think he may have even convinced himself; But when the time came for our relationship to move into more intimate circumstances, he shied away. One night I came over to hang out with him and watch television and he sat on the far end of the couch, nowhere near me. Eventually we drifted apart because he couldn't commit to me. He just was not ready. The sad part is, if we had waited a while I think we may have been able to date, but we acted much too quickly.

—*Amanda K.*
  Berkeley, California

THE FIRST TIME I MET MY EX-BOYFRIEND'S mother, she deliberately pointed out the "M" on my ex's University of Michigan baseball cap, a hat he always wore, and told me that the "M" stood for mother and that she will always be the No. 1 woman in his life. She told me this in front of his entire family during the first week we were dating. I knew then that the relationship was going to be a challenge.

> —*N.L.*
> *NEW YORK, NEW YORK*

. . . .

ONE TIME I WAS IN A BAR and I asked this guy out for the next day. The next day we met and we walked around and met some of his friends and sat down to have ice cream. I asked him these questions and all of a sudden he put down his spoon and said, "You think I'm a guy, don't you?" Even gay guys get it wrong sometimes. I learned to always make sure of the gender before investing the money in ice cream.

> —*PATRICK CLIFTON*
> *SAN ANTONIO, TEXAS*

. . . .

I WENT ON A FIRST DATE WITH SOMEONE who showed up a half-hour late, covered in dirt, limping, and hung over. He ran into me at the place we were supposed to meet. He had been hurrying home to change; he thought he still had an hour until our date. But then he saw me and realized. I said, "So, what happened?" And he told me this story about how he was drunk the night before and fell down and sprained his ankle. That was pretty much how the date went. I called my friends and had them come get me out of it. It was odd.

> —*ANONYMOUS*
> *BALTIMORE, MARYLAND*

SIGNS OF THE PSYCHO

1) Jealousy
2) Over-protectiveness
3) Paranoia

—*COSI SMITH*
BURKE, VIRGINIA

If he lets you drive but tells you when to shift, just pull over to the side and let him out.

—*J.*
SAN JUAN, PUERTO RICO

LET'S *NOT* GET PHYSICAL

EXTREME POSSESSIVENESS, JEALOUSY, wanting to know where you are at all times—they're all signs of a relationship that could turn physically abusive. A lot of times it starts with verbal abuse before it gets physical. Once the verbal abuse starts it's a very slippery slope down to physical abuse. And the best thing to do is get out while it's still just verbal abuse, because the guy who is that way is never going to change. He may hit you and say, "Oh, I'm sorry I'll never do it again." But he's gonna do it again. I dated a guy who was very abusive. It was one of those situations where he'd say, "If you ever leave me, I'll kill you." It started slowly and it worked its way up until one day I realized that I needed to get out of there. I went to my folks and told them I wanted out; they came down and got all of my stuff. And I basically disappeared for five or six months.

> —*ANONYMOUS*
> *WASHINGTON, D.C.*

* * * * * * * *

MY FIRST RELATIONSHIP WENT BADLY because he was crazy and manipulative. He was nice and polite in front of my parents but totally different when they weren't around. He was in the Navy. He got out by pretending to be suicidal. I was in community college and he was trying to convince me to get married ASAP. Finally I just realized he was nuts. I mean, I was too young to be thinking about marriage. If we got in an argument and I tried to break up, he'd start crying and say I was his life. When I finally did break up with him, he continued to call me in the middle of the night, when I was asleep, to see what was going on. He was very jealous of all my friends, guys and girls, and he didn't want me to see any of them. I came very close to filing a restraining order against him. I pretty much had to cut all ties with him even though he wanted to stay friends and kept calling me. I had to tell him to never call me again.

> —*ANONYMOUS*
> *SEATTLE, WASHINGTON*

I WAS FRIENDS WITH THIS ONE GIRL and we ended up going to the movies together. And after the movies we hooked up, and then we started dating. Things were going great but I found out later that she would spy on me. I was bartending and she would send her friends in to check on me to see if I was flirting. And she would drive around and look in the windows of the bar to see what I was doing. I really liked her and I had never cheated on anyone and never gave her signals that I would. But she became an obsessive-compulsive stalker. The funny thing is, about a year after we broke up she had moved to another city and she called me. She said she met this guy that reminded her of me. And she ended up marrying that guy.

—*J.S.*
  ATLANTA, GEORGIA

• • • • • • • • •

IF HE WON'T LEAVE YOU ALONE, send him things he doesn't need. I had a psycho ex-boyfriend who tormented me with his calls, frequent surprise visits, and gifts. For a period of two or three months he wouldn't leave me alone and wouldn't take 'no' for an answer. It was a nuisance more than anything else. My roommate and I got the brilliant idea to reward him for all his attention by sending him some presents. So one Sunday we sat down with the Sunday paper and subscribed him to a variety of interesting magazines (Computer World, Better Homes and Gardens, Playgirl and Readers Digest, to name a few). We also sent away for all those great little trinkets that they offer in the Sunday inserts, choosing the "send it now/bill me later" option to make life easier for him. He received an Elvis commemorative plate collection, really stupid looking miniature porcelain dolls, and a small electric eggbeater. All very useful things. This is probably mail fraud—but harassing someone is a crime, too, so I figure we're even.

—*S.G.*
  NASHVILLE, TENNESSEE

If a relationship is too exciting, try to stay away from it. It might end badly. It's sort of like the "you don't get anything for free" kind of thing.

—ANONYMOUS
CLARK A.B.,
PHILIPPINES

I HAD SOMEONE TAKE ME TO HIS HOTEL room for a first date. We sat on a heart-shaped couch and watched free porn. Guys, don't try that with girls on your first date. We'll just assume you're trying to sleep with us.

—KAYZE
BALTIMORE, MARYLAND

· · · · · · · ·

WE GOT HALFWAY THROUGH OUR MEAL and I guess he felt like he could now divulge his deepest secrets to me, because he said, "I frequent this psychic and she told me that in a past life, I was Moses." I was certain I'd misunderstood him. Then he leans across the table and says, "I went to this same psychic just before our date to see what she thought of you. She told me you'd have a significant influence on my life." So I leaned in and said to him, "Think you can get your money back?" He just sat there and looked at me as I stood up, put down cash for my meal, and left.

—PENNY C. SANSEVIERI
SAN DIEGO, CALIFORNIA

· · · · · · · ·

ON MY DATE FROM HELL, the guy firmly believed that if you had nothing important to say, you should say nothing. So he said nothing.

—JEN W.
SAN CARLOS, CALIFORNIA

· · · · · · · ·

ASSESS THE CONDITION OF YOUR DATE on arrival. I went on this one date with a guy, and I didn't realize it at first, but he was drunk. We got to the restaurant and I began to see that he was not very coherent at all. He laughed at one point and this stream of liquid came out of his nose. I excused myself to go to the ladies room and walked out of the restaurant.

—LEILA
WASHINGTON, D.C.

Dead End: Breaking Up, Moving On

Why do you even date, anyway? If it comes down to this— breaking someone's heart or, worse, having yours broken— isn't it just easier to refrain from relationships? Too late. You're in a bad relationship, and you're going to leave it one way or another. And remember to pencil in some time to recover. Here's what happened to others, and tips for the aftermath.

IF YOU CARE ABOUT THE PERSON, there is no nice way to break up. If you cared about the relationship, there is no easy way. If it wasn't a meaningful relationship, then the only way is to be totally brutally honest and fast.

—*PANOS KOUTSOYANNIS*
SAN FRANCISCO, CALIFORNIA

I'VE NEVER BEEN THE CRAZY EX-GIRLFRIEND. I'M IN THE QUICK-RELEASE PROGRAM.

—*KATE*
ATLANTA, GEORGIA

Avoid the Reunion Tour: that's the post-break-up smooching. It gives false hope.

—*ALLIE R.*
WASHINGTON, D.C.

THE MORE DEVELOPED I HAVE BECOME as a person, the less upsetting a break-up is. You realize that things happen for a reason, and you allow your-self a bit of time to heal, and then move on. Make sure you are over the ex, though, before you start a relationship with someone else. That's the worst mess-up ever.

—*ANONYMOUS*
NEW YORK, NEW YORK

•••••••••

BE RATIONAL WHEN BREAKING UP. Understand when it's just not going to work. As soon as you've gone through two rounds of break-ups with a person, don't go through a third. It didn't work out twice for a pretty good reason.

—*Z.K.*
MINNEAPOLIS, MINNESOTA

•••••••••

YOU KNOW THE RELATIONSHIP'S OVER when you start going around and around on the same issues and nothing gets resolved. After the first three months, some argument always comes up. It's either going to be a lasting problem or some-thing you can resolve. If you don't resolve it, you know it's over.

—*BARBARA*
OMAHA, NEBRASKA

•••••••••

IF YOU THINK ABOUT NOT BEING WITH HIM as much as you think about being with him, that is a big problem. Relationships are a choice, and there are so many people that you could be with. I never understand why anyone would settle for anything less than perfect!

—*JENNY B.*
NEW YORK, NEW YORK

DON'T WASTE TIME ON GUYS who don't treat you the way you want to be treated, or make you over analyze yourself or the relationship. I dated a guy for way too long who didn't treat me like I was worth anything, and it made me feel awful. The only reason I stuck with it was because I was afraid of breaking it off with him and then not finding anyone better. This is a terrible reason. If you are having these thoughts, run for your life. There is always someone better, even if it takes a while to find him or her. Everyone deserves the opportunity to be with a person who treats them well.

—BRONLEA HAWKINS
BELLINGHAM, WASHINGTON

I remember the following: Hurt me once, shame on you. Hurt me twice, shame on me.

—OLIVIA
CASTLE ROCK,
COLORADO

A MATTER OF TRUST

Trust your partner, or else! My girlfriend used to always suspect that I was cheating. Every time my phone rang, the girl would get all paranoid and need to know who it was. It drove me crazy. And it bothered me so much, it became a self-fulfilling prophecy! I DID cheat.

—N.K.
NEW YORK, NEW YORK

Pay attention to how a girl you're dating acts when you're out with her. If she's really into getting a lot of attention from other guys at a bar, for instance, I think, "I can't trust that one. If she's like this when I'm with her, what is she like when I'm not?"

—BILL BRAZELL
BROOKLYN, NEW YORK

I DON'T KNOW WHICH IS WORSE, breaking up or getting broken up with. It's just part of life. Suck it up. If you are dumping someone, you have to do the whole "it's not you, it's me" thing, even if it was them. Even if you're planning to be honest, the words "it's not you, it's me" will just slip out. And that's OK. It's the best way to play it.

—*TIM*
   SCOTTSDALE, ARIZONA

• • • • • • • •

❝When I break up with people, I say the usual things. "This isn't working out. I feel like I need to grow. I need to experience other things.' ❞

—*ANNE*
   WILMINGTON, NORTH CAROLINA

• • • • • • • •

Admit nothing, deny everything.

—*B.W.*
   NEWPORT BEACH,
   CALIFORNIA

WHEN I'M NOT INTERESTED IN SOMEONE, I make it as obvious as possible in my attitude towards them. I can be really condescending, standoffish, and sometimes vulgar and obscene to the point where she gets completely offended. I think it's better that way than making someone feel rejected. I'd rather make her think that she's not interested in me. I find it easier than rejection.

—*ANONYMOUS*
   IOWA CITY, IOWA

I HAD A DRAGGED-OUT BREAK-UP with a boyfriend. We dated two years, and we were on and off for a whole year. At first it was the summer of my discontent, and then it turned into fall, winter and spring of my discontent. Sometimes break-ups aren't black and white. You really care for the person, but there are some things you can't work through or accept in the relationship.

—*KAREN S.*
SACRAMENTO, CALIFORNIA

I DATED A GUY FOR A YEAR and it was amazing. I was going to marry him. And then he broke up over the phone—over the phone! I was like, "If you're a man, you'll come here and break up with me to my face." Then he came over and we made out that night. Then we hooked up twice the following year, and he gave me a urinary tract infection. Then I saw him out with someone else, and I was actually calm. I went up to him and I said, "Hey, what's up?" And he wouldn't even acknowledge me. He had never done that before. I started fuming. I couldn't believe he was doing that. The next thing I knew, my drink was out of my glass and all over him. It made me feel very liberated.

—*ROBYN*
ATLANTA, GEORGIA

Become an expert at the break-up talk. Saying, "I'm just not feeling the chemistry I want to feel," is the best line, as it's true and unassailable.

—*AMOL DIXIT*
MINNEAPOLIS,
MINNESOTA

ONE OF MY GIRLFRIENDS BROKE UP with me by e-mail. Don't ever do that to a guy. It was bad because I wasn't able to get a real explanation from her. All she said was, "We are broken up, goodbye."

—*YONI OINOUNOU*
WASHINGTON, D.C.

FRIENDS TILL THE END— AND BEYOND

I'D ACTUALLY BEEN QUITE IN LOVE WITH THIS ONE GUY, but even after he dumped me, we both said we really wanted to try to stay friends. My birthday came not too long after that and I told him he didn't need to get me anything, but he said he wanted to and made a big production of giving it to me. It was a CD of his new girl-friend's band. Honestly, is that the worst gift or what? Needless to say, we're not friends anymore. If you're going to stay friends with an ex, don't rub their face in your new relationship.

> —*KAMMY T.*
> *SAN FRANCISCO, CALIFORNIA*

YOU CAN NEVER BE FRIENDS WITH AN EX. The person who got dumped always wants to be friends because there is that hope you'll get back together. The per-son who did the dumping may be friends out of guilt, but that is always dangerous.

> —*B. GOLDSTEIN*
> *BUFFALO GROVE, ILLINOIS*

YOU CAN TOTALLY BE FRIENDS WITH PEOPLE YOU DATED. But you do have to get past the whole dating thing first. I dated a guy for two years, and then we broke up. But we still saw each other through friends. And then a year later, when we were dating totally different people, and we started talking again and we became good friends.

> —*JUSTINE MOJICA*
> *ATLANTA, GEORGIA*

TAKE IT FROM AN EX-GIRLFRIEND who knows: The only reason guys ever want to remain friends with their exes is so they can get friendship sex during the dry spells.

> —*ERICA NAGEL*
> *DEERFIELD, ILLINOIS*

I THINK YOU HAVE TO BE WILLING to give a little more of yourself, to do things that you might not necessarily be interested in. My girlfriend and I had some divergent interests. She was more of the tree-hugging, Birkenstock-wearing, granola type, and I was more the sports type. About a year ago, she started going to these dance classes, and I went with her some of the time, but not often, because I didn't expect her to come with me when I played tennis. Well, she met somebody there. One day she came home and said, "I met somebody who has a lot more in common with me and I'd like to give it a whirl."

—*ANONYMOUS*
PHILADELPHIA, PENNSYLVANIA

• • • • • • • •

IN ELEMENTARY SCHOOL, if I wanted to break up with a girl, I would've been mean to her and wait for her to break up with me. As an adult, you just have to be honest. Just say, "It's been fun. But I don't think we're heading into marriage so we should probably just be friends." Give her a hug and hopefully she accepts it and you can still be friends.

—*MIKE*
STRAFFORD, NEW HAMPSHIRE

• • • • • • • •

IF A GUY IS DUMB ENOUGH TO BREAK UP with you in the first place, don't give him the time of day! My first serious boyfriend broke up with me on our one-year anniversary, but still had a plane ticket to come and see me in Europe for a month. He came, stayed with me at my house and I was trying to get him back the whole time. I found out he was calling his new girl-friend all the time on my phone bill.

—*LAURA*
IOWA CITY, IOWA

Don't pine over someone you've broken up with. It ended for a reason. Remember, you can love someone, you can miss some-one, but you can still be better off without them.

—*TEENA HAMMOND GOMEZ*
CORONA, CALIFORNIA

A while later, in a new relationship with the terrific man who I later married, I realized that breaking up really isn't a bad thing—it's an opportunity to upgrade!

—*Anonymous*
New Tripoli,
Pennsylvania

DUMP HER IN PERSON. It makes you feel terrible— no one likes to make a girl cry. But you have to do it face-to-face. I would never do it by e-mail or a letter or phone. I would do it face-to-face out of respect even though it's definitely the hardest way.

—*N.S.C.*
Marietta, Georgia

• • • • • • • •

IT'S HARDER TO DUMP. If you're getting dumped, you don't have anything to lose so you can just sit there and smile and hear what their excuse is going to be. If you are doing the dumping, the burden is all on you to do it delicately and try to come up with a reason that's not so contrived or trite that it's insulting. I don't think I've ever heard a good reason. You either have to be trite and say, "It's not you, it's me," or you have to be honest and be hurtful. If you're honest, there are few reasons to break up that won't hurt the other person. I guess you try to find a happy medium. There's no ideal way to do it.

—*R.M.*
Athens, Georgia

• • • • • • • •

HOW DO I HEAL FROM A BROKEN HEART? I work out a lot, write, and play with my dog: pretty much the same thing I do every day except I'm depressed and it lessens a little bit with each passing week. That's until I hit the cynical stage, when I usually go have some adult beverages with friends and get kind of catty and snide, with a heavy dose of humor, to release any excess anger.

—*Sarah*
Des Moines, Iowa

APRIL FOOL

My ex-boyfriend's birthday is April 1 and mine is April 9. For his birthday, I surprised him by inviting his best friend from out of state to our apartment for the weekend, and I paid $250 for the plane ticket. You'd think he would have wanted to spend time with his best friend, but he wanted to drink instead of palling around. I tried to leave the two of them alone, but his friend kept asking me to come along. His friend thanked me for showing him a good time, but I never received a thank-you from my ex. On my birthday, I didn't get anything—not even a card—and he was late meeting me for dinner.

To make matters worse, a week or so later, he threw a party for another girl who "never had a good birthday," and he wanted her to have something special to remember. That's probably what ended it for me.

—JENNIFER STURM
IOWA CITY, IOWA

I'D RATHER DUMP SOMEBODY than be dumped—at least you know when the end is coming. You can feel like you had the last word. Then again, if you get dumped, you don't have to feel guilty.

—BRENT MOSLEY
ELLIJAY, GEORGIA

• • • • • • • •

MY EX-HUSBAND IS OF A DIFFERENT RELIGION and it caused a lot of problems. I think it was because he was such a hypocrite about it. He used his religion when it suited him. So after that, I would never date someone who didn't have the same beliefs as me.

—B.D.
STUTTGART, GERMANY

There's an "I'm Sad" phase. Then there's the "I'm Angry" phase. Then there's the "I Need a Rebound" phase. Make sure you skip that last phase.

—K.
LAKEWOOD, TEXAS

MAKE FRIENDS WITH THE FAMILY of the person you're dating—they can save you from heart-break. I was engaged to this girl who was living in Colorado with her grandmother while I was stationed in Ft. Lewis, Washington, on active duty for the Army. Because of my schedule, we some-times went for months without talking, so I didn't always know what was going on with her. One day, her grandmother, who adored me, called me out of the blue and told me she was preg-nant—with someone else's baby! In the span of a couple of months (and, more significantly, behind my back), my girl-friend moved to Alabama to live with the guy who'd impregnated her, realized he was a complete ass, had an abortion and moved back to Colorado. She had no idea her grandmother told me any of this, so when she returned to Colorado she called me up and innocently asked, "When are we getting mar-ried?" Needless to say, my answer was, "Never."

—JADE PHOENIX
CENTENNIAL, COLORADO

YOU MIGHT LOVE SOMEONE, but you know it's time to take a break when you're having more bad times than good times. You go to a bar, you get in a fight. You're not enjoying each other's company. When that happens, it's time to leave.

—*CRYSTAL*
BREMEN, GEORGIA

• • • • • • • •

I'VE ALWAYS BEEN THE ONE TO DO the breaking up even though I have typically been the passive person in the relationship. Sometimes the only control I have ever had was the strength to say that it's over.

—*SARAH*
SEATTLE, WASHINGTON

• • • • • • • •

WHEN IN THE MIDDLE OF A BAD BREAK-UP, always consider two things:
1) The things that are best for you are sometimes the things that are the hardest to do.
2) Act in a way you'd be able to accept unflinchingly one year from now.

—*CHRISTINA*
BELMONT, MASSACHUSETTS

• • • • • • • •

A FEW YEARS AGO, I was in a long-term relationship with a total jerk. When we broke up, my boss, who was a good friend of mine and had observed the relationship and break-up, asked me, "What are you going to learn from this?" I thought about it for a minute and answered, "I'm going to learn not to date jerks!"

—*ANONYMOUS*
NEW TRIPOLI, PENNSYLVANIA

It's always sad when you and your girlfriend break up around Valentine's Day, but eating the giant box of candy you'd already bought for her helps somehow. It's therapeutic.

—*K.*
INDIANAPOLIS, INDIANA

What helped me after the heartbreak was just sitting and crying my eyes out.

—*STEVE "DICK" SPENNEBERG BEVERLY HILLS, CALIFORNIA*

HOW TO HEAL FROM A BROKEN HEART? Of course, as with anything there's giving it time, but I also found that music, drinking, venting, dry heaving and confrontation helped me through a great deal of pain. That, and good friends to pick me back up and set me straight.

—*JEFF ELLIS CROSS LANES, WEST VIRGINIA*

• • • • • • • •

TO GET OVER A BREAK-UP, go on a manic shopping spree. That usually helps. And it's more fun if you use your ex's credit card.

—*GABRIELLA PHILADELPHIA, PENNSYLVANIA*

• • • • • • • •

CAN'T BUY ME LOVE

The craziest thing I've ever done is essentially try to buy a girl back. I showed up at her house with like four dozen roses, put her in a car, drove her to where we had a hot air balloon ride, drank champagne on the way there. A limousine picked us up after that and took us to a comedy club, where I sprung tickets to Mexico on her. She wanted to go and she did love me, but she said she couldn't commit to me. That whole thing was a big turning point for me. I called up the travel agent, changed names on the reservations, and I ended up having an all-guy trip to Mexico. I don't have any regrets about the girl. It was a wonderful date even if it was our last. And I ended up having a great time in Mexico.

—*TRAVIS WIDNER ATLANTA, GEORGIA*

ONE OF THE HARD THINGS ABOUT BREAKING UP is losing a family you really love. I was so close to my ex-boyfriend's parents and sister. We'd been together for several years and everybody assumed we'd get married—including us. His family was so sad when we broke up, his parents and sister both called me. They said they wanted me to stay in their life, but it's just too hard and awkward. And then, of course, once I met another boyfriend, whom I ultimately married, it got even weirder. So I never see them anymore, which is sad, because they were like a second family to me.

—*S. COLEMAN*
NEW YORK, NEW YORK

• • • • • • • •

THE WORST BREAK-UP I EVER HAD happened when this guy I'd been seeing for nearly four months just stopped calling me out of the blue without any explanation. Up until that point, I'd thought things had been going great. For several weeks, I tried calling him and even stopping by his apartment, but he completely avoided me. It was pure torture because I never saw it coming. To this day, I still wonder what happened!

—*LEAH SCHULTZ*
CASTLE ROCK, COLORADO

• • • • • • • •

HAVE CLOSURE. SAY GOODBYE. I just had someone break up with me. It blindsided me. He was a nice guy. I think it was fear of commitment. It's so weird how it was done. He left all my things in a paper sack on his front porch. No note, no call. I called twice, he never called back. It was the last thing I ever expected. He never contacted me. Because it's such a mystery, it's a shock.

—*SCOOTER STRINGER*
SAN FRANCISCO, CALIFORNIA

> Just know that you are a goddess, and if he can't see that, then he is a waste of your time.
>
> —*ALLISON B.*
> *BOULDER,*
> *COLORADO*

In a break-up, sex is always the last thing to go.

—*Anonymous*
Placerville,
California

DON'T GO OUT AND GET DRUNK when you're trying to get over a break-up. Go out and get laid. I'm trying to get over a girl. It's been a week. I got drunk the other night and that's not going to make me feel better. Nothing makes you feel better about getting over somebody—at least if you're a guy—like sleeping with someone else. Especially if that person is more attractive than the person you're breaking up with.

—*Richard*
Atlanta, Georgia

• • • • • • • •

" **The biggest rule in helping a friend through a break-up: No drunk dialing! Take her phone away from her, delete her ex's numbers and make sure she doesn't go home with the first person who shows interest in her.** "

—*K.*
Lakewood, Texas

• • • • • • • •

HEALING FROM A BROKEN HEART happens in stages. First, I'm sad and a little angry with myself. Then there's the wild party and strip-club stage. Then there's dating or going out with another woman. Finally there's reflection and lessons learned and laughing at the fun stuff.

—*Sugar Johnson*
Brooklyn, New York

WHEN HEALING FROM A BROKEN HEART, make effigies and burn them! (Just kidding.) I write in my journal and talk with my friends. I have faith that the pain will go away and it always does.

> —J.A.
> DURHAM, NORTH CAROLINA

• • • • • • • •

THE BEST THING YOU CAN DO FOR A FRIEND who's going through a break-up is go over to her house, rent a movie, get a pizza. Just be there. Rent those love-story movies. "You've Got Mail" is one of the greatest movies of all time; it restores your hope. And you think, "Tom Hanks would never cheat on me! That's the kind of man I need!" It'll make you cry more, but that helps you get through it.

> —JULIE THRIFT
> TAMPA, FLORIDA

• • • • • • • •

THE BEST WAY TO HEAL FROM A BROKEN HEART is to spend time with yourself. Figure out all of the things that you like, not the things that you, as a couple, liked. There are lots of differences, and I rediscovered a lot of things that I had forgotten about as I merged my taste with someone else's.

> —SARAH
> SEATTLE, WASHINGTON

• • • • • • • •

THE WAY TO GET OVER A BREAK-UP is to focus on all the little day-to-day things that you do. Don't think about what they might be doing or what they could be doing because then you're going to find yourself in their world and not your own. Focus on your own small world and stay within that world because anything outside of that is dangerous.

> —STEVEN GROSS
> MANCHESTER, GEORGIA

I always tried to soften my break-ups as much as possible, but I learned that sometimes a little brutal honesty is actually kinder than it seems.

> —N. CLARK
> HOUSTON, TEXAS

Nothing says, "Go away" like a flaming bag of dog poo or some well-placed rotten eggs.

—CHRIS VANDERBILT
CASTLE ROCK,
COLORADO

I SURVIVED MY BREAK-UPS BY STAYING BUSY. I stay busy from the second I wake up until I crash at night. I get over it by talking to my friends, talking to random people, going out, dancing, being crazy, meeting new people.

> —MICHELLE
> DAYTON, OHIO

• • • • • • • •

DO NOT PERSONALIZE REJECTION. This is key. You are not less of a person if it does not work out. Your value needs to come from inside you, not from a date. Dating is about trial and error—don't internalize it.

> —ANONYMOUS
> MONTCLAIR, NEW JERSEY

• • • • • • • •

WHAT REALLY GOT ME THROUGH MY BREAK-UP was my spirituality. I trusted that there was somebody out there for me and it was in God's hands. What's meant to happen will happen.

> —LIZ
> ATLANTA, GEORGIA

• • • • • • • •

HOW DO I HEAL FROM A BREAK-UP? Well, trite as it sounds, time does eventually do it. I have yet to find a faster, more effective way to go about this. Of course, there's always ice cream and chocolate—temporary fixes help too.

> —KRISTEN J. ELDE
> SEATTLE, WASHINGTON

• • • • • • • •

✓ **IF YOU'RE WAFFLING,** go on one more date. If you're still waffling, cut it off or else you go out three weeks longer than you should have or wanted to because you didn't have the balls.

> —TIM SMITH
> MINNEAPOLIS, MINNESOTA

DEAR HEARTBROKEN:

Don't panic. Don't start second-guessing everything he ever said to you, thinking, "Oh my God, he lied to me. He said he loved me, but he never meant it. Everything he said was just to trick me into caring about him and trusting him … just so he could screw me over."

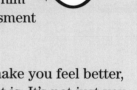

Understand that he meant everything when he said it. He wasn't lying. He wasn't trying to ruin you, his motives didn't have anything to do with you (typical selfish male). He just didn't realize that you thought love lasted forever. Don't stay mad at yourself. Soon you won't think about him the same way; soon you won't feel embarrassment every time you run into him.

Search for break-up advice online. It won't make you feel better, and all the answers will be crap, but the point is: It's not just you. Everybody feels worse than they'd like to for longer than they should.

Invite all your friends to a bonfire on the beach, burning all his pictures and everything he ever gave you, so you can symbolically rid yourself of his bullshit. It might not make you feel any better, but it'll be fun. And then don't tell him about it; that way, you have a secret you're keeping from him. The next time he asks you, "Oh, by the way, do you still have that [insert whatever thing he might ask about]?" you can just laugh at him and he won't know why.

—L.

I HAD A HORRIBLE BREAK-UP. I got over it by keeping really busy. I took that time to improve myself. I took on hobbies. I started doing triathlons. I had always been a runner but had been slacking in that area. So I started spending more time doing those things, getting in shape.

—*LORRAINE*
TAMPA, FLORIDA

66 The best way I have found to deal with having your heart stomped on is losing yourself in a good movie. A Hitchcock film festival and a one-pound bag of peanut M&M's is my alternative to Paxil or Prozac. 99

—*SHAWN M. GREEN*
MELBOURNE, FLORIDA

HOW DO YOU GET OVER A HARD BREAK-UP? Movies help. Working helps. Drinking helps. Random hook-ups really help. Listening to Lou Barlow also helps: There's some good advice on Sebadoh's *Bubble & Scrape*. After a while, after enough break-ups, you realize life goes on. Someone new always comes around.

—*LEE*
BROOKLYN, NEW YORK

I GOT THROUGH IT BY NOT REACTING TO HIM, ignoring everything he did. I spent lots of time with friends and family and just threw myself into my work. I spent hours and hours making pottery and keeping as busy as possible. Anytime I felt weak I would just push the bad thoughts out of my head and think of all the positive things in my life.

—*JACQUELINE MUELLER*
ATLANTA, GEORGIA

TO GET OVER A BREAK-UP, try to do things that you enjoyed while you were with the person that didn't involve the person. Just do stuff that is solely you. That always makes you stronger. Everything passes with time, no matter how much it hurts. And it does hurt.

—*KEIRSTIN*
FINDLEY, OHIO

NO DOUBLE DIPPING! Once you break up don't go there again; don't go back to him. You'll never meet anyone new and you always end up going back to your old guy. It's not worth it, so keep moving forward.

—*COURTNEY CRAIG*
SAN DIEGO, CALIFORNIA

IF YOU'RE TRYING TO GET OVER AN EX, don't have a one-night stand with a girl that looks like the girl who just dumped you. That does not help. That just makes you horny for the girl who dumped you.

—*ANONYMOUS*
TOPEKA, KANSAS

If you want to know if a guy is good for you or not, ask your dog; dogs sense things that people don't. If the dog wags its tail, he's probably a good guy. If the dog growls, head for the hills!

—*CINDY PFEFFER*
FOREST HILL,
MARYLAND

SHOW SOME MERCY when you're breaking up with someone. I had a boyfriend dump me on Christmas Eve; then we got back together, and he dumped me again on Valentine's Day. As he broke up with me, the second time, he reiterated how much he'd like to stay friends. Yeah, fat chance of that.

—*CHRISTINE B.*
NEW YORK, NEW YORK

"If he wants to see you for lunch, that's the end. He's just going to break up with you, otherwise he'd be making a date for a weekend night. So why have lunch? Tell him you're busy and you'll call him when you're free. But don't."

—*N.*
BROOKLYN, NEW YORK

IF YOU'RE NOT THAT SERIOUS with somebody, and don't want to be, try just letting a relationship die a quiet death. I used to think that was somehow immature, but I've found that a few unreturned phone calls get the point across without having to do the cliché, "It's not you, it's me" routine. I've done it and had it done to me, and I have to say I've found it preferable to a big break-up scene that would be inappropriate for a little relationship.

—*SEAN H.*
NEW YORK, NEW YORK

I WISH I KNEW HOW HARD IT would be to break up with my boyfriend once we were living together. I've always operated under the dating philosophy that I will stop dating someone when I know I couldn't marry him. This is the first boyfriend that I've lived with, and I've learned some things about him and how we communicate (or don't) that I couldn't have known before we lived together. Now I don't think I could marry him, and yet I can't bear the thought of breaking up with him. Since he was the one who moved into my apartment, a break-up would mean he moves out. But the thought of his stuff not being in my place, or how empty the spare room would be, is not a happy thought.

> —ANONYMOUS
> CALIFORNIA

. . . .

I JUST STOPPED SEEING A GIRL I've been dating for a couple months. We got along great and were compatible, but I just didn't feel anything for her in my heart. My heart didn't skip a beat every time I saw her and I didn't think about her constantly. I plan on getting married once and only once to a person I could not live without.

> —ADAM ROEDERER
> LOUISVILLE, KENTUCKY

. . . .

COMMUNICATING IS THE MAJOR FOUNDATION of a relationship. If you can't convey your feelings, you're going to screw it up. I dated a girl who wanted me to serenade her. She wanted me to send her notes. She wanted me to write her poems. I had just known her for two weeks. She never communicated her needs to me until they built up. She told me when we were breaking up, four months later.

> —R.K.
> NEW YORK, NEW YORK

Don't play games with people. If you don't see yourself with that person, end it. And stop it earlier rather than later.

> —KATE MOYNIHAN
> MINNEAPOLIS,
> MINNESOTA

HEALTHIER TO HATE?

It's better to hate someone than to have mixed feelings about him or her, at least according to a recent study. How do the researchers explain these surprising findings? If you hate someone, you avoid that person. But if you still have hope for friendship and support, you may be setting yourself up for disappointment.

WHEN SOMEONE DOES YOU WRONG, get revenge. When I discovered a long-ago boyfriend had lied to me about another girl, I emptied his shampoo and conditioner bottles and refilled them with vegetable oil. I still smile when I remember how bad his hair looked for the next week. (Oil doesn't wash out of hair overnight.)

—*LESLIE*
BEVERLY HILLS, CALIFORNIA

• • • • • • • •

THE PHRASE "LET'S JUST BE FRIENDS" should be permanently retired. After a long relationship, no one wants to "just be friends." Feelings of love and hate don't go away easily. So distance yourself from the one who drives you nuts instead of creating a friend who drives you nuts.

—*TRAVONNIE N.*
FRANKLIN, TENNESSEE

More Wisdom: Good Stuff That Doesn't Fit Anywhere Else

S*till seeking more advice? You could try your Magic 8-Ball, or you could read on. Sometimes, navigating the world of dating calls for a unique perspective. We asked, and people delivered. Will you find what you're looking for? Signs point to yes.*

THE BEST DATING ADVICE I EVER HEARD was "be yourself." So who else could I be? Tom Cruise? If you can be Tom Cruise, be Tom Cruise: you'll probably have more success.

—*DAVID ARENSON*
JERUSALEM, ISRAEL

WOMEN ARE ATTRACTED TO THE MEN THEY LOVE. MEN LOVE THE WOMEN THEY'RE ATTRACTED TO.

—*KIM*
JACKSONVILLE, FLORIDA

LOVE IS LIKE ANY OTHER HOBBY: If you want to be good at it, you have to practice every day. Sure, you're going to mess up; it's how you deal with it that determines the outcome. I say, overcome your failures and keep going. If you think constantly about how you can improve, and then you do it, you will only get better at whatever it is you want to, especially when it comes to love.

—*EDDIE P.*
SAN DIEGO, CALIFORNIA

NEVER DATE A WORKAHOLIC who says he will have more time for you in the future. I dated a guy who held several jobs and was always working. I thought he would change, but I got sick of waiting around for him.

—*A.F.*
CHICAGO, ILLINOIS

IT'S OK TO TELL YOUR FRIEND if you have a problem with his significant other. I dated a girl once who was a compulsive liar—she told me that she worked as a U.S. Boxing ring girl in Tokyo and Mexico City, that she was crowned Miss Missouri and that she held the record for selling the most Girl Scout cookies in the entire country. My friends were too nice and didn't say anything until I realized it myself. But I wish they had told me.

—*ANONYMOUS*
IOWA CITY, IOWA

KNOW THE PERSON WELL. Observe him in many situations. Watch what happens when he is angry. See how he treats waiters and cab drivers. Look for character, because that's what you will rely on later.

—*A.N.P.*
PITTSBURGH, PENNSYLVANIA

AN OPTIMIST LAUGHS TO FORGET. A pessimist forgets to laugh. You have to go into a relationship with high hopes. Always try to see the best in people, or they won't look for the best in you. And try to remember that dating should be fun.

> —CINDY PFEFFER
> FOREST HILL, MARYLAND

JUST ENJOY THE DATING SCENE. I spent so much time worrying about whether every guy I met was "the one." I didn't just enjoy getting dressed up, putting on makeup, and going out for the evening. I examined and re-examined every word my date said to find out if he loved me and whether he was marriage material. When I finally became exhausted with that process, I just enjoyed dating someone. I changed my expectations and really began to have fun. That's when I met "the one." We got married the following year.

> —STEPHANIE
> NEW YORK, NEW YORK

DON'T PUT LABELS ON THE RELATIONSHIP. I try to stay away from the "boyfriend" and "girlfriend" labels and have had great experiences—but I can only date really independent and secure women.

> —MATT
> NEW YORK, NEW YORK

DON'T START DATING TOO QUICKLY after your divorce. I was so happy to be out of the marriage that I immediately started dating. But I started dating men who were just like my former husband. I needed time to re-discover myself, but I didn't take that time.

> —LINDA
> SEATTLE, WASHINGTON

Pick the person for who they are and not what they do or earn. Jobs and money status change, but the person stays the same.

> —KIRAN
> ATLANTA, GEORGIA

Always date redheads.

—*NICK S.*
NEW YORK,
NEW YORK

HAVE FUN! Date as many men as possible—not only the nice ones. You need to experience all kinds of men before settling down with a nice man. Just try not to get into any real trouble. But most of all, have fun so you can look back and smile. It was important to me to be able to tell my daughter about my fun dating experience and give her advice about it.

—*E.G.*
NEW HAVEN, CONNECTICUT

• • • • • • • •

❝Don't date two different guys with the same name at the same time. If one of them gives you a gift "from Todd," you might call the wrong person to say thank you.❞

—*LAURIE C.*
DENVER, COLORADO

• • • • • • • •

JUST HAVE FUN WITH IT. Life, especially dating, shouldn't be so serious. Hey, you get a few free dinners—at the very least, a few free drinks and a couple of first kisses. But don't put all this pressure on yourself, thinking on a first date, Oh my gosh, is he the one? You'll end up just disappointing yourself.

—*ERIN CAMPBELL*
SAN DIEGO, CALIFORNIA

MESSAGE: BE YOURSELF

NEVER GET IN OVER YOUR HEAD IN ORDER TO BAG A HOTTIE: it's just not worth it. For an entire summer I had a crush on a guy who finally asked me out. He was one of those raft guides whose job was to float tourists down a river. When he invited me to go kayaking with him down a Class-4 river, I was a little hesitant, but I agreed because he was so hot. Making matters worse, I accepted the "medicinal" cigarette that was being passed around that day. Paranoia turned to panic when I saw the first rapid looming on the horizon. It was large, white, and angry-looking. For the next three-and-a-half hours, I sucked in what felt like half of the water in the river and proceeded to lose one of my paddles. It was horrible! And it was not just me and my date on this wacky water ride. As he picked me up that morning, he mentioned that four of his buddies would be joining us. He hoped I didn't mind. I did.

—*LEIA*

• • • • • • • •

DON'T LOSE YOURSELF OR WORRY ABOUT WHAT THEY THINK OF YOU! Drastic changes don't need to happen. Just take it one day at a time and remember who you are; it is much better in the end.

—*MARY JOHN FRANK*
NEW YORK, NEW YORK

• • • • • • • •

IT'S TAKEN ME A LONG TIME TO REALIZE that for any relationship to work, whether platonic, romantic, and passionate, it's essential that I be myself within that relationship.

—*JENNY WHITE*
MALDON, VICTORIA, AUSTRALIA

Never listen to a girl after she confesses to cheating on you. She will inevitably break up with you, claiming that it's not for the other guy—and end up with the other guy.

—*A.M.*
INDIANAPOLIS,
INDIANA

EVERYONE MAKES YOU THINK that there is one person you're supposed to be with for the rest of your life. What they forget to tell you is that there's also at least one psychopathic maniac. You should figure out who the person that you're with is, because many people mistake the psychopathic maniac for The One.

—*JENNIFER ZBOZNY*
PITTSBURGH, PENNSYLVANIA

• • • • • • • •

DON'T LET YOUR EYES GET IN THE WAY of your head. I've botched more attempts at love with women I find extremely attractive physically than with others I find more attractive in other ways. Had I approached the physically attractive ones with my eyes closed, it might have worked out a little better.

—*BRAD*
CHICAGO, ILLINOIS

• • • • • • • •

I THINK WITH ALL THE RELATIONSHIPS I've been in, I've grown as a person. I've learned good things through dating these people. It allowed me to experience things I might not have. I gained self-confidence in who I am and knowing what I am. Now I know what I'm looking for.

—*MICHELLE*
DAYTON, OHIO

CREDITS

Pages 6 and 14: Elaine Fantle Shimberg, Author of *Another Chance For Love? Finding a Partner Later In Life*

Page 17: Sperling's BestPlaces, 2004

Page 24: Sperling's BestPlaces, 2004

Page 28: www.filmsite.org

Page 44: www.MSN.com

Page 58: MSNBC: May 12, 2004

Page 60: Study by the Institute for American Values, reported in Chronicle of Higher Education

Page 63: MSNBC: May 12, 2004

Page 65: Evan Marc Katz, Founder of Dating Consulting service E-Cyrano.com, and author of *I Can't Believe I'm Buying This Book: A Commonsense Guide to Successful Internet Dating*

Page 83: Brian Caniglia, www.DateSeeker.com

Page 87: © Copyright www.RomanceStuck.com, 2000-2004

Page 91: www.webmd.com

Page 95: www.AllAboutMoms.com

Page 98: www.Butlerwebs.com

Page 120: www.whyfiles.org, July 12, 2001

Page 127: Knowledge Networks, for AARP The Magazine, June 2003

Page 131: World Health Organization, 2003

Page 168, 169: www.ivillage.com Relationships

Page 200: Health Psychology, Journal of the American Psychological Association, quoted on www.webmd.com

HELP YOUR FRIENDS SURVIVE!

Order extra copies of *How to Survive Dating*.

Check your local bookstore or order here.

Please send me _____ copies of How to Survive Dating.

Enclose $12.95 for each copy. Add $4.00 for shipping and handling for one book, and $2.00 for each additional book. Georgia residents must include applicable sales tax. Payment must accompany orders. Please allow 3 weeks for delivery.

My check for $_____ is enclosed.
Please charge my __ Visa __ MasterCard __ American Express

Name _____

Organization _____

Address _____

City/State/Zip _____

Phone _____Email _____

Credit card # _____

Exp. Date _____Signature _____

Please make checks payable to HUNDREDS OF HEADS BOOKS, INC.

Please fax to 212-937-2220, or mail to:

HUNDREDS OF HEADS BOOKS, INC.
#230
2221 Peachtree Road, Suite D
Atlanta, Georgia 30309

HELP WRITE THE NEXT Hundreds of Heads™ SURVIVAL GUIDE!

Tell us your story about a life experience, and what lesson you learned from it. If we use your story in one of our books, we'll send you a free copy. Use this card or visit **www.howisurvived.com** *(indicate 'referred by BRC').*

Here's my story/advice on surviving

❏ **DATING**   ❏ **MARRIAGE** (years married: _____)

❏ **FRESHMAN YEAR** (college and year of graduation: _____)

❏ **A NEW JOB** (years working:_____ profession/job:_____)

❏ **A MOVE** (# times you've moved:_____) ❏ **A DIET** (# lbs. lost in best diet: _____)

❏ **A TEENAGER** (ages/sexes of your children: _____)

❏ **DIVORCE** (times married: _____) times divorced:_____)

❏ _____ **OTHER TOPIC** (you pick)

Name _____City/State: _____

❏ Use my name ❏ Use my initials only ❏ Anonymous

(Note: Your entry in the book may also include city/state and the descriptive information above.)

How should we contact you *(this will not be published or shared)*:

email: _____ other: _____

Please mail to:

HUNDREDS OF HEADS BOOKS, INC.
#230
2221 Peachtree Road, Suite D
Atlanta, Georgia 30309

Waiver: All entries are property of Hundreds of Heads Books, Inc., and may be edited, published in any medium, etc. By submitting content, you grant Hundreds of Heads Books, Inc. and its affiliates a royalty-free, perpetual, irrevocable, non-exclusive right (including any moral rights) and license to use, reproduce, modify, adapt, publish, translate, create derivative works from, distribute, communicate to the public, perform and display the content (in whole or in part) worldwide and/or to incorporate it in other works in any form, media, or technology now known or later developed, for the full term of any Rights that may exist in such content, and to identify you (with the information above) as the contributor of content you submit.

Your story/advice:

_____

_____

_____

_____

_____

_____

_____

_____

_____

_____

_____

_____

_____

_____

_____

_____

_____

_____

_____

_____

_____

_____

_____

_____

_____

_____

_____

_____

_____

_____

_____

ABOUT THE EDITORS

MARK BERNSTEIN runs a private equity firm working with early-stage technology and media companies. He is a graduate of the Wharton School of Business of the University of Pennsylvania and New York University's School of Law. After a career as a lawyer, Bernstein was a senior vice president of CNN and general manager of CNN's digital content division, CNN Interactive (CNN.com). Bernstein is a veteran of many years of dating... having experienced both the good and the bad. He claims to hold the single season record for blind dates. His friends and family are thrilled that he now has the advice of "How to Survive Dating" and he is sure that, armed with the advice of HUNDREDS OF HEADS, "this is the year."

YADIN KAUFMANN is a founder of a venture capital firm that invests in high-technology start-up companies. He received his AB from Princeton University, JD from Harvard Law School, and AM from Harvard's Graduate School of Arts and Sciences. He dated his future wife, Lori Banov Kaufmann, for 5 years, and has written two books with her, including *The Boston Ice Cream Lover's Guide*—which taught them that the key to a great relationship is dessert.

VISIT WWW.HOWISURVIVED.COM

Do you have something interesting to say about marriage, having a baby, holding a job, dating, or one of life's other challenges?

 Help humanity—share your story!

 Get published in our next book!

 Find out about the upcoming titles in the HUNDREDS OF HEADS™ survival guide series!

 Read up-to-the-minute advice on many of life's challenges!

 Sign up to become an interviewer for one of the next HUNDREDS OF HEADS™ survival guides!

Visit www.howisurvived.com today!

Other Books from HUNDREDS OF HEADS™ Books

HOW TO SURVIVE YOUR FRESHMAN YEAR . . . by Hundreds of Sophomores, Juniors, and Seniors Who Did (and some things to avoid, from a few dropouts who didn't)™
(April 2004; ISBN 0-9746296-0-0)

HOW TO SURVIVE YOUR BABY'S FIRST YEARS . . . by Hundreds of Happy Moms and Dads Who Did (and some things to avoid, from a few who barely made it)™
(December 2004; ISBN 0-9746296-2-7)

HOW TO SURVIVE YOUR MARRIAGE . . . by Hundreds of Happy Couples Who Did (and some things to avoid, from a few divorcees who didn't)™
(February 2005; ISBN 0-9746296-4-3)

HOW TO SURVIVE YOUR TEENAGER . . . by Hundreds of Still-Sane Parents Who Did (and some things to avoid, from a few whose kids drove them nuts)™
(Spring 2005; ISBN 0-9746296-3-5)

HOW TO SURVIVE A MOVE . . . by Hundreds of Happy Dwellers Who Did (and some things to avoid, from a few who haven't upacked yet)™
(Spring 2005)